# WORLD LOCKED IN

Six Weeks in Coma
and Beyond

*To Bonnie –*
*Thanks for you friendship and*
*support. Hope you enjoy!*
*Best,*
*Mark*

## Mark Hathaway

Quinlo Publishing

*Designed and produced by*
Maine Authors Publishing
558 Main Street
Rockland, Maine 04841
www.maineauthorspublishing.com

Printed in the United States of America

*I* dedicate this book to my mother, Louise Quinn Hathaway, not only for her love and care while I lay in a coma and suffered from Locked-in Syndrome, but also for supporting me during my recovery. Without her assistance transcribing, typing and editing, this book may not have become a reality.

# Chapter 1

# Slipping Away

The ambulance doors swing wide. The attendant riding in back with me slides the stretcher toward other attendants, poised and ready for the relay. With one swift movement, they rush me through the Emergency Room doors. The crisp, clear air of the fall morning fades, replaced by the antiseptic odor and fluorescent lights of the emergency waiting room.

All eyes focus on the body being wheeled forward. It is my body that everyone is watching, and I am embarrassed by the attention.

"He's young," a voice says, surprised.

"He must have been in a car accident," another voice responds. Somehow I feel I am disappointing them; no blood, no gore.

I begin to writhe and squirm with fever. The sheet on my stretcher is damp with sweat as I burn from within. Nurses in white glance down at me as they scurry past.

I have embarked on a grueling personal odyssey, all within my own mind and body.

The ambulance attendants wheel me behind a curtain. The female EMT leans over and speaks distinctly in my ear, as though I do not understand English. "We'll leave you here. You'll be in good hands. Doctors will be with you soon."

The attendant makes last-minute checks to see that I am secure. She seems reluctant to leave me. As she goes, her world, the one to which I am accustomed, will slip further from my grasp.

*"Let your mind drift, do not be afraid," a voice is saying. The old man sits cross-legged like a jade Buddha on a puffy cloud suspended in space, the earth far below him.*

*"Have I been here before?" I ask myself.*

*I begin to travel through time, and enter a glorious, gilded pavilion with a vaulted ceiling: the Hall of Ancestors. I picture myself as a young boy. My grandfather presides, and my grandmother sits beside him. Silence fills the vast hall as the images of ancestors flash by like holograms, appearing and disappearing.*

"Mark," a voice interrupts. "Mark, how are you doing?"

Picasso could have painted the face peering down at me. The cubistic shape, with one eye much lower than the other, introduces itself as Doctor Stand.

"Do you have any idea what happened?" he asks, but I cannot speak. "Here's a pencil and paper. Can you write your answer?" That simple question snapped me back into reality and caused me to focus on recent events and to explain how I landed on the examining table.

It all had begun Sunday, three nights earlier. A group of us had eaten dinner at a Korean restaurant in Evanston, where the food was very good. The restaurant looked clean—unlike some of the restaurants I'd visited in Seoul a year earlier, where it had taken liberal shots of Korean rice wine to make the raw fish, kimchee, and rice palatable.

After dinner, we all returned to the fraternity house where several of us were living. I was attending the Kellogg Graduate School of Management at Northwestern University in Evanston, Illinois. My room was large, quiet and surrounded by the rooms of other graduate students.

*Shogun* was on television that Sunday night. The Japanese outlook on life, death and reincarnation that the show presented intrigued me, especially the idea that death could be the first step into a new life. At midnight, when the telephone rates to Canada dropped, I called my girlfriend Lisa in Montreal, where she had recently entered McGill University. We had met two years earlier in Toronto, lived together in Taiwan, and traveled around the Far East and Southeast Asia. We'd both cried when I told her I had decided to enter graduate school in the Chicago area. With Lisa in Montreal and me in Evanston, our relationship would be strained, but everything seemed fine as we talked about my booking a flight to Montreal in a couple of weeks.

After the phone call, as I was preparing for my first day of classes, my head started to ache. The dull pain in the back of my head rapidly worsened, so I put aside the accounting book I was reading and decided to take two Tylenol.

The walls seemed to spin as I got up from my bed. I dismissed my poor balance, thinking that I'd stood up too quickly after reading lying down. My headache grew so severe that I dropped down on my bed again, laying my head on a pillow and afraid to move at all.

*Is this what a migraine is like?* I wondered. *Maybe I'm worried about the first day of classes, and reading all this accounting has given me a migraine. I don't know why in hell I'm doing this, anyway. I never did like to study. How could I ever forget what school is like?*

For hours I lay there, afraid to move my head from side to side. My paranoia grew. Business school! What would these people be like? Certainly it would be different from living on a beach in Thailand, where Lisa and I had had such a good thing going just months earlier. My thoughts flashed to Ko Samui, where we had rented a bungalow on the beach, romped in the waves, and feasted on fresh fish, papaya, and mangoes.

When I got up to go to the bathroom, I noticed I was beginning to lose strength and felt sick to my stomach. I waited for my headache to subside, but by three o'clock that morning, I was too sick to read all my accounting homework before my nine o'clock class. It was time to get help.

My new friend Wesley, who lived on the same floor, liked to stay up late. I stumbled to his room, using the walls for support. My head throbbed. My balance was even shakier than before. I held my head as motionless as possible, but that proved difficult with the walls spinning around me. My brain felt like it shifted painfully within my skull with each step.

A crack of light appeared from beneath Wesley's door, and I knocked as hard as my dwindling strength would allow. Wesley looked surprised when he opened the door. I had liked Wesley, an American-born Chinese from San Francisco's Chinatown, as soon as I met him. Bright and relaxed, he had a sharp sense of survival and liked to play poker. Now, he looked puzzled.

"Wesley, can you help me?" I asked, each word jarring my brain.

"Sure." He looked concerned. "What can I do for you?"

"Will you call the student infirmary? Tell them I have an incredible headache and ask them what I should do," I said.

Wesley helped me to the pay phone down the hall. In no time, he was talking with a nurse at the University Infirmary. "He has a severe headache and feels nauseated. He doesn't look too well. No, he hasn't been drinking," Wesley said. I lost track of the conversation.

Leaning against the wall for support, I held my head in my hands and hoped for relief from the pain in the back of my skull.

"How long has this been going on?" he asked, bringing me back into the conversation.

"About three hours," I whispered, trying to minimize any movement.

Wesley finished his conversation with the nurse, and turned back to me. "Just to be safe, she's sending over a campus policeman to take you to the Evanston Hospital Emergency Room," he said. "He's coming right over."

By the time Wesley helped me down the stairs and outside, the police car had already arrived. Between the front door of the fraternity house and the car, I vomited three times.

"Had a little too much to drink, did you?" the policeman asked as he aimed me toward the pail on the floor. I realized he had made similar trips to the Evanston Hospital, and assumed I was just another student who could not hold his liquor. Still afraid to move my head, I ignored the question and stared directly ahead.

The emergency room looked empty when I arrived. The clock on the wall said that it was 3:25 a.m. When the receptionist noticed my arrival, she put down her sandwich and started to ask questions.

"Name. Address. Type of insurance."

I gave her my name and told her that I was covered by the student health plan at the University. My head was pulsating, and I quickly grew impatient with the questions. What was I doing in the hospital, anyway? What could they do for a headache? At least it would give me a good reason not to go to Accounting class.

A young female doctor led me to an examining table, her inexperience obvious. Under normal circumstances I might have been more inclined to invite her to dinner the next Saturday than to listen to her prognosis, but now I welcomed any help.

After questioning and probing, the doctor could not find anything wrong with me. Eventually, I fell asleep. When I awoke two hours later, the pain had eased, and although I was still weak, the young doctor released me.

"If the pain continues, go to the University Infirmary and they'll help you there," she said.

For the next two days, I left my room only to go to the bathroom across the hall. I had planned to go to my Business Management class on Monday afternoon, but after waking up around noon, I decided to rest and wait until the next day. I was waiting to hear what Wesley and the others had to say about the first day of classes, and whether any of the professors had noticed my absence.

By nightfall my headache had grown worse, and there was sweat on my brow. People who stopped by told me I was not looking well. On Tuesday morning I had no energy to go to class, and just wanted to stay in bed.

"I've never had a headache last this long," I told Wesley.

When my friend Sam came by on Tuesday afternoon, it was easy for him to convince me that I should go to the University Infirmary. At least there, I would be adequately fed. I had been surviving on the dried fruit and nuts left over from my cross-country drive to Northwestern a week earlier. I was less concerned about the growing pain in the back of my head, or my inability to maintain my balance when I stood, than with the prospect of another meal of gorp. Also, I trusted Sam's judgment. I had only known him a week, but we had become good friends. Both of us were new to Northwestern and had a Maine connection. We depended on each other for support.

On arriving at the student infirmary, I was ushered in to see a doctor. She saw that I had a fever, but she could not accurately diagnose my problem. As she assigned me to a bed, the squint in her eyes revealed her concern.

"Possibly you're suffering from the after-effects of that head cold you just had," she explained. I was in no mood to pose any argument. By this time, I just wanted to lie down.

Once in bed, I felt increasingly uncomfortable and withdrawn. When the nurse brought my dinner, I could manage only two bites. The fever was making it difficult to concentrate and next to impossible to converse with visitors. The dull pain in the back of my head weighed more and more heavily with each passing hour, and by nightfall I drifted into a doze. During the night, I finally mustered the strength to make my way to the bathroom.

Spinning walls made it difficult to stand. My weak legs could no longer support me, and I dropped to the floor. I reached for the buzzer on the wall to summon the nurse, but my arm felt leaden and would not respond. I wanted to rest before trying again, and melted into a heap on the floor tiles, where I lay until a nurse found me the next morning.

"How did you get down there?" the nurse asked.

I searched for words that would explain what I was doing on the bathroom floor, but they would not come. My body felt drained of strength, and as the nurse helped me back into bed, I did not think about what had happened. I was concerned only with reaching the comfort of the sheets. I was like a child who had fallen asleep in a car. The only thing on my mind was to fall back to sleep.

When the sun rose, I could hear voices. "I thought it was more than a cold. I could just see him burning up."

"So what happened?" someone asked.

The nurse explained how she'd found me on the floor.

"He's so weak he can't even speak," the unknown voice said.

As she helped me onto a stretcher, the female ambulance attendant smiled and assured me that everything would be all right. I closed my eyes and tried to assure myself that everything would be fine. When I opened them again, I had returned to the Evanston Hospital Emergency Room where I had visited Sunday night, but this time I lay on a stretcher.

As Doctor Stand, the man with the cubistic head, examined me, voices on the other side of the curtain distracted me. "He just kept hitting me," the female voice cried. "I was afraid he was going to hit the kids. He's lost his temper before, but not like this."

"It's OK. You're all right now," a voice said.

"What will you do when you leave here?" another voice asked, and I heard more sobbing.

*I don't need to listen to this. How did I wind up here?*

My major concern was getting out of the hospital. Never having been in an emergency room before Sunday night, I was not comfortable in the surroundings.

It was now mid-morning, and the emergency room was buzzing with activity. In the background I still heard voices.

"Bring him in here," a doctor said above the crowd. "Now, let's take a look at that leg."

"It doesn't look too good does it, Doc?"

"How did you do this?" The doctor asked.

"I tripped in a hole running."

There, that's what emergency rooms are for, broken bones. What am I doing here with a headache? Why all the fuss?

Doctor Stand leaned forward, his face appearing much larger than his frame could support. He seemed to sense an emergency, but he remained composed, as I imagined a stewardess might act before an airline disaster.

He said slowly, "We're going to give you a CAT scan now. This lady will take care of you."

As orderlies wheeled me to the X-ray area, I studied the nurse who was going to take care of me. Her close-cropped hair and sharp features gave her a stern appearance that made me uncomfortable. It might have been her stiff, technical air or the sterile, futuristic surroundings of the CAT scan area, but I thought of George Orwell's *1984*. I wanted to leave as soon as I entered the room, but I lay helplessly on the stretcher, unable to speak and too weak to move.

The helplessness increased as the orderlies placed me on a cold, metal slab and strapped my head into a helmet-like device that kept my head from moving. Panic swelled, and I struggled in vain to free myself as the orderlies left the room.

A voice echoed over a loudspeaker. "Now, you have to lie very still. This won't take long."

I waited for Vincent Price's eerie laughter, but it never came.

With a whir, the metal table receded into the wall. My head entered a crypt-like opening and kept moving back. My struggle continued. I stared wild-eyed around me. Was this really happening? I tried to maintain my composure and remain still while the painful pressure in my brain increased until it felt ready to explode.

The picture-taking started, and continued and continued. Every few seconds, with a muffled sound like an engine far across the water, film would be advanced: click, click, click. The table would move forward ever so slightly, and the process would start all over again.

*What are these people looking for? Maybe they are searching for my mind!*

The voice scolded me over the loudspeaker. "Come on, now, you must lie still."

I started to scream, but could not utter a sound. I shut my eyes tightly and set my jaw, wondering if the ordeal would ever end. I remained still and patient for an eternity.

At last it was over. I could finally move my head and breathe some air. I had been suffocating. I was claustrophobic, trapped in a mine only large enough for me.

The orderlies wheeled me to the Intensive Care Unit, but I could not understand why. *I'm not that sick*, I told myself. *Why does everyone make such a big fuss over me? If everyone will just leave me alone, I'll get well.*

I was slightly dazed upon arriving at ICU, but I felt reassured by the sight of nurses going about their daily routines. They were relaxed, competent, and composed people who had been through all this before. Their calm, businesslike approach suggested that they believed, as I did, that I would soon get well.

Although I imagined that I was on the fifth or sixth floor, I pictured a normal, everyday scene going on outside. I saw cars passing by a church, and people filing into the church, and was later very surprised to learn that there was no church below.

The neurologist entered my room with his assistants, and started reflex tests. He poked me with what seemed to be a safety pin, checking my reactions. When he rubbed the bottom of my foot, I realized my reflexes were slow. I still did not believe I was ill, and wanted a chance to prove myself. When he tapped my knee with a reflex hammer, I was prepared. As quickly as I could, I kicked my lower leg out as if it were a normal reflex action. He was not fooled. I was searching for a way to prove to all these strangers that I was a healthy twenty-five-year-old male.

Soon after the doctor left, Dean Wilson, the Dean of Students at Northwestern's Kellogg Graduate School of Management, arrived. I recognized him immediately. I had seen him give a welcoming speech to new students the week before.

"Hi, Mark. I've called your parents and they're on their way."

This seemed an unnecessary imposition on my parents, since I was not really sick, but I felt relieved and reassured. My parents could put an end to this nonsense and get me out of this place. If I could make it until they arrived, I would be in capable hands.

Although Dean Wilson looked relaxed, I sensed his concern. It troubled me. If he was concerned enough to summon my parents from Maine, maybe I was sicker than I realized. For the first time I wondered if I might be seriously ill.

"They said to let you know that they would call your brother and sister and girlfriend," Dean Wilson said. *Why would my parents call Lisa?*

*What the hell is happening to me?* I wanted to scream. I didn't believe they would contact her directly unless something was seriously wrong.

The day that had started clear and crisp was now gray and cloudy. Wind blowing off Lake Michigan rattled the windows. The fluorescent overhead lights in the room contrasted with the approaching darkness. The night I feared was arriving. I fought drowsiness. My parents had not arrived yet, and I would try to wait until they came before I closed my eyes and slept.

Darkness, the unknown, was frightening. My eyelids felt leaden. If I shut my eyes I might lose control, so I concentrated on keeping them open. I was facing the night alone.

As hospital activity slowed, and the inevitable darkness arrived, my thoughts drifted off. I was in a dreamlike state, but this dream was more intense than any other dream I had ever had. I felt as if my body had been transposed to another time, another place.

*I'm in a race. The fraternity where I'm living is in a competition with a nearby "macho" fraternity. Cockiness envelopes our opponents, and my dislike for them grows. The race becomes a drinking contest, and I will be the human sacrifice if we lose. We struggle to keep up, but they are slowly pulling ahead. I'm drinking beer so fast that I'm gasping for air. Each time I drink beer, I come up gasping. We are losing the race, and I can only remember that I am the human sacrifice.*

As someone entered my room, I snapped out of my dream. It was dark, and the hospital had grown quiet. I tried to forget my dream, but my mind was still racing. Images flashed: the race, gasping, footsteps. My body no longer seemed connected to my mind. I was losing my grip on reality, and felt helpless to stop it.

I struggled to find a thought that would comfort me. I felt as though I floated in a vast ocean at the mercy of the waves, and scanned the horizon for an island where I could find refuge. In the distance, breakers crashed against rocks revealing land, but the swells blocked it from my view, and I continued to float powerlessly. Eventually, waves washed me onto a beach, where I lay exhausted.

*If I can only make it through the night, my family will be here tomorrow, and then everything will be back to normal.*

The nurse who had entered my room and saved me from my dream told me to press the buzzer whenever I needed attention. She fluffed my pillows to make me comfortable. Before she had time to leave the room, I pressed the buzzer. She held my hand and seemed to realize the torment I was experiencing. Her hand was warm and friendly and caring. The warmth of her hand was the reality I needed.

"That's OK, Mark, you're all right," she assured me. "What can I do for you?"

I just lay there, unable to speak, my muscles too weak to move. Each time she got up to leave the room, I pressed the buzzer. I was terrified of being left alone. Never before had I experienced such fear. I did not want that warmth, that only piece of reality, to leave. Only her presence could stave off the encroaching darkness.

For the next few hours, each time she left, the nurse would say, "I have to go, Mark, I have to go. I have another patient to watch." But as soon as I was left alone, fear would strike again. Petrified, I was trapped in my mind with horrifying dreams of death and eternity. The nurse always returned, the warmth of her hand was comforting, but she could not prevent my journey into the unknown, and once again I entered a dream-state.

*I am in an East Indian hospital. The conditions are very crowded, and one patient after another dies. As each patient dies, a pretty, young Indian nurse covers the corpse with a white sheet. She slips me a note. The note reads, "If you want to survive, pretend you are dead."*

*I close my eyes and lie very still. I hear the nurse's delicate footsteps and imagine her dark, seductive body walking toward me. She raises the soft cotton sheet over my head.*

## Chapter 2

# Dancing Elephants

"Hi, Mark, we're here. Everything will be all right now."

The familiar voice woke me. It was my brother John. John knew, like no one else, the relief I experienced when I heard familiar voices. He also seemed to know how reassuring it was to me to hear that everything would be all right. We had often marveled at the fact that we were thinking the same thing at the same time. When we played chess, I often felt we could anticipate each other's strategies because our thinking patterns were similar. John usually won those games, not because he was that much better than I, but because he had his status as big brother to protect.

We'd always had a competitive relationship, and in addition to his three-year age advantage, he tried a little harder to avoid being humiliated by his little brother. I always wanted to beat him, but on those rare occasions where I was victorious, it was not fully satisfying. I liked having a big brother I could trust and emulate.

Growing up, I was always in John's shadow, both physically and mentally. Physically, John was always large for his age. Like many younger brothers, I would tag along with him and his friends. Five or six inches taller than I was and about fifty pounds heavier, John was an excellent athlete. I could never match his athletic feats. The weight of my brother's reputation daunted me. In grade school, teachers would call me John. I did not look that much like my brother, but that was their first word association with Hathaway. Some days I cursed the fact that I was the youngest Hathaway, while other days it made me proud. I learned early on that

I lived in his shadow.

Other people were standing in the room with him. Curious, I tried to open my eyes, but they would not open. The previous night's fear was gone, replaced by calm and serenity. Not bothered by the fact I could no longer open my eyes, I had reached another level of consciousness and was content to stay at that level. My mind drifted effortlessly.

*Lying in the soft sand, I feel the warmth of the sun on my body. A gentle breeze caresses me while waves break on the shore. Muffled voices call me in the distance. I hear a seagull and picture the blue sky. My eyes are closed, but I still sense the bright sunlight. Relaxed, I am in no hurry to move at the sound of my name.*

Two warm lips kissed me on the cheek. I knew those lips well. It was my girlfriend Lisa. She held my hand, but said nothing.

I later learned that my father had reached her at school in Montreal and said that I was very ill. Having talked with me only three nights earlier, Lisa was not sure how serious my illness could be. She later told me that she had called her own mother, an occupational therapist, who said, "If you ever want to see Mark again, go to the hospital." On the plane trip to Chicago she had rehearsed what she would say, but standing beside my bed, seeing my still body, she was speechless.

Circumstances bound Lisa and me closely together. After graduating from college, I had worked in Toronto, where my brother had opened two eateries. Lisa worked at one of the restaurants, and came to my rescue on several occasions. I was new to the city, and she had graciously shown me around town. She was so pretty, with her sparkling blue eyes, but she was only eighteen when we first met, and I made the mistake of underestimating her beguiling powers.

Lisa was having problems at home and was in a very rebellious stage. Fiercely independent, she distrusted all males, including me, but once I gained her trust, she was a powerful ally. One night while gazing at the moon, I kissed her, and from that moment on, ours was a passionate love affair.

I had gone to Toronto to save money for a trip to East Asia. I had no expectations that I would meet a girl and fall in love. I had known Lisa for six months when I went to East Asia as originally planned. After finishing school in the spring, Lisa had joined me. We lived in Taiwan, where

I taught English to Chinese businessmen, soldiers, and students. I also earned money as an English-speaking liaison for an import-export company and as an extra in Taiwanese movies. In the movies, I was one of the token whites, but it helped pay the bills and was always a good time. In one movie, I was a judge in a boxing match; another time, I was a villain in a Kung Fu movie; and I was also a Vietnam-era soldier on a television series.

We rented an apartment with an American friend whom I had met earlier, and Lisa found a job tutoring. In a city that was exciting and foreign to us both, we depended upon each other for support.

We had lived together in Taipei four months when we decided we had saved enough money to tour other countries in the region, and we flew to the Philippines. Two weeks after our arrival, we found ourselves on an island several hours away from Manila, where we met Jim. Although the village was a small, picturesque fishing hamlet, we wanted to find a more remote island—the main requirement being that it have a nice beach.

Our friend Jim told us of another island which he described as the most beautiful of the 7,100 islands making up the Philippine archipelago. Jim had fallen in love with the Philippines while serving two years in the Peace Corps sixteen years earlier, and had not yet left. Jim had traveled throughout the islands, and Boracay surpassed all the others with its fine, white sand beach that stretched for four palm-tree-lined miles. The only people sharing the beach with us would be fishermen casting their nets.

"Go there," Jim said. "You won't be disappointed."

Early one morning, Lisa and I loaded our backpacks on a Jeepney. Jeepneys are colorful World War II vintage jeeps, draped with tassels, mirrors, and pictures of Jesus, and modified to carry passengers. Indigenous to the Philippines, they are the principal means of transportation on the islands. We traveled on gravel roads that wound through valleys and jungles, the air heavy with moisture. In Pandoro, we were to catch a bus to the opposite end of the island. By the time we had finished eating, the temperature had already reached ninety-five degrees, and the humid air was stifling. People stared curiously at Lisa with her blue eyes and white skin as we loaded our backpacks onto the bus and sat back on a rear seat.

Once loaded with passengers and sacks of flour and rice, the bus headed south. The gravel road we traveled was full of potholes, but at least it was level, where earlier the road had twisted up and down hills. Two hours later, the bus jounced into a small village for a rest stop, where the arrival of the bus seemed to be the big event of the day. Everyone stopped whatever they were doing and stared as we disembarked.

The village was small and dusty, typical of an Asian village coming into the modern age. The barefooted villagers wore jeans and T-shirts emblazoned with the names of American universities. The traditional way of life—fishing and farming—seemed incongruous with the truck parked at the mechanic's garage across the street. A sign in disrepair advertised ESSO gasoline.

After eating some rice and fresh fish at a village café, Lisa went to find an outhouse while I looked after the packs. Before Lisa reappeared, the driver started the engine and was off. I jumped onto the bus and still saw no sign of Lisa.

"Stop! Stop!" I yelled, reaching for our belongings. As I was about to throw our packs off and jump after them, I saw Lisa reappear and start sprinting. The driver slowed, and I reached out to help her onto the moving bus.

"I can't believe that guy!" Lisa said.

"He must be nuts!" I responded.

"What would we have done in this little village?" she gasped.

We both looked back at the small, quiet Philippine hamlet. We thought of the heat and swarming flies and imagined where we would have slept until the next bus arrived on the scene.

"We would have managed somehow," I said, silently wondering how.

With the bouncing of the bus and the humidity, Lisa eventually leaned against my shoulder and fell asleep. Lazily, I watched as the Filipinos went about their daily activities. Some tended water buffalo and cows, while others worked in the fields planting rice or tended children. They all glanced up as the bus traveled down the dusty road. I wondered why their houses among the palm trees were constructed on stilts. *Was it because of high water during the rainy season, or to avoid snakes and rodents?* I shuddered at the thought.

After two hours, the bus descended into a dry riverbed, and we literally hit the ceiling when the bus bounced into the first of many huge potholes. As we landed back on the wooden seats, the Filipinos chuckled. All the locals were sitting at the front of the bus, where the ride was much smoother. With broad grins, they beckoned us forward. At sunset, we finally arrived exhausted at our day's destination, the village at the southern end of the island from which the ferry left for Boracay.

The boat to Boracay left twice a week. If all went well, it would leave the next morning with Lisa and me aboard. We found a hotel room, and at seven the next morning, hired a motorized rickshaw. We rode out to the beach where the boat had anchored for the night.

The boat did not inspire confidence, to say the least. Thirty-five feet long, the narrow wooden boat sat low in the water some twenty yards offshore. It was old and decrepit, and I wondered how we could still read its name, *Serpent*, on the stern. Black smoke poured from a five-inch smokestack. I could hear its engine rumbling, and then saw one of the crew wearing a tattered T-shirt and carrying a wrench in his hand. My confidence rose slightly as I noticed a wooden pontoon out-rigged on one side. At least the pontoon would give the boat some stability.

"I don't know about this," Lisa said, mirroring my concerns.

"Oh, we'll be all right," I assured her, trying to convince myself at the same time. "What do you want to do now, go back the way we came?"

"Why do you always get us into these predicaments?" Lisa asked, as if it were all my fault. "Here we are on some beach four miles away from some tiny village in the middle of nowhere!"

I sat in the sand, pondering our future. At least the weather was good and the water looked calm. I got up to speak to the boat captain, and learned that the boat did not sail directly to Boracay. First it crossed the Minoray Strait to Lorca, another island in the Philippine archipelago. The boat would anchor there for the night before going on to Boracay the following day. The fare would be twenty pesos, or about three dollars, for the four-hour trip to Lorca.

"They want us to sleep overnight on that boat," I reported.

"No way, not on that wreck. Can't we sleep in the village tonight?"

"The boat anchors in a harbor away from the village," I explained. "I say we just take the boat across the strait. We can always get another boat to Boracay, if we don't want to stay with that one. It's not that much further, and there are a lot of boats that travel between these islands."

Two hours after the boat was scheduled to depart, porters began to load cargo, mostly sacks of grain and huge clusters of bananas. By the time Lisa and I were shuttled out to the boat in a small dugout canoe, the skies had grown threatening. It was common, in the 7,100 islands, for a sunny day to transform into a raging tempest. We took refuge in the cramped cabin and sat down on a wooden bench. The passenger cabin was only five feet high, with three benches stretching the width of the cabin. We could hear water sloshing in the bilge below.

After half an hour at sea, rain obscured any sight of land, and the wind was strengthening. The engine strained against the growing force of the waves, and the boat pitched with each one. "Don't break down now," I prayed. The boat had no radio, no lifeboats, and no life jackets—not that life jackets would have helped much in the shark-infested waters.

"I can't stand being in here," Lisa said. "I'm going up above. At least up there I can get some fresh air." Waves were breaking against the starboard side of the boat and coming through the wooden shutters of the porthole. None of the portholes had any glass, and with each wave a torrent of water shot into the cabin and down into the bilge.

"How are you ever going to get up there without being washed overboard?" I asked, not ready to part with the relative security of the wooden bench.

"I don't know, but I can't stay here," Lisa answered. "I would rather be up there if this boat goes down than cramped in here."

I looked around at the other passengers: fourteen in all, including Lisa and me. The only one that appeared to be weathering the storm well was a fighting cock that one of the men carried. The three-man crew was sitting in the cockpit drinking a local gin straight from the bottle and eating raw fish. The passenger sitting beside me vomited, covering my pant leg. Other passengers were becoming ill.

"Let's get out of here!" I said.

The boat was riding with its deck barely a foot above the surface of the water. The wind whipped the rain and the spume, but the fresh air was a relief after the stench below. An old woman lay under a tarpaulin, somehow managing to hold on. She was too ill to worry about us, and seemed to have her own method of braving the squall, one that we were not ready to disturb. Lisa and I crawled to a wall that would offer some protection. Exposed to the elements, we huddled together and clutched a halyard that was used to tie down supplies.

*Is this what it's like for the Vietnamese refugees?* I wondered. I felt like vomiting, but if I was going to drown, I wanted to do it with dignity, not miserably throwing up over the side of the *Serpent*. I had no intention of dying on a hulk in the middle of the Minoray Strait. Lisa and I held on to each other tightly and prayed. At times, I thought I could feel her heart beat.

The trip that was to last four hours lasted nine, but with Lisa at my side, it was bearable. The storm finally subsided as we approached land,

and we gratefully waded a quarter mile to shore as the sun was setting. Two days later, we continued our trip to Boracay on another boat, and found the island even more idyllic than Jim had described.

As Lisa held my unresponsive hand that September afternoon, she knew I was going to need her help through another crisis.

"Do you think he can hear us?" The whisper came from a third person in the room, my brother's wife, Suellen. Like Lisa, she was from Toronto and supportive.

I heard my parents' voices as they entered the room. They sounded troubled, but tried to maintain control. The only person missing now was my sister Nancy, nursing her newborn baby—my parents' first grandchild—in Rhode Island.

I still didn't know what was happening to me, but I was confident that with my parents, Lisa, John, and Suellen there, I could make it through anything. My doubts had disappeared. My mental condition was improving. I was no longer slipping away.

"So, how is he doing?" Mom asked.

"You're going to be OK, aren't you, Mark?" my brother answered for me.

"You'll be well in no time," my father said.

"You've got to hurry and come to Montreal," Lisa said. "We're having a big party in a couple of weeks."

They all had decided for me that I had to get well in a hurry. Having little to say in the matter, my plans switched from "if I recovered" to "when I recovered." I had to get well soon. As in the Philippines, the bus might slow down, but it would not stop.

Lisa held my hand, but got no return pressure from me. "It just isn't fair," she said.

"We were up to Diane's in Bangor this weekend when we got the call," Mom said. "The foliage is really starting to change."

After an awkward pause, my brother asked, "How is Diane doing?"

"She's doing well. That's a nice little apartment she has up there."

Another pause. "How is your house coming in Baltimore?" Mom asked.

"We're working on the roof. We hope to have it done next week," John said.

"They are finally building that brick wall out back," Suellen said.

"How do you like McGill, Lisa?" Mom asked.

"It's OK, but I guess I miss Mark a lot," Lisa said.

My mind started to drift away from the conversation. It was increasingly difficult to concentrate, but I was not sleeping; I was overwhelmed by an intense daydream.

*As I ride a big white stallion down the empty street of a city, people are leaning out of windows of high buildings. They look puzzled. A woman in a long black dress scurries out of one of the buildings to meet me. She lifts her veil and I lean down, expecting a whisper. "Don't you know?" she says. And it echoes in my ear.*

"Let's get some lunch," my father suggested, waking me from my dream. I had missed much of the conversation.

"I think we should take turns staying with him so he is not alone," John said. "I'll stay with him first. Why don't you pick up a sandwich for me?"

I was relieved that I wouldn't be alone. If I were left alone, I might begin another slide. I needed people with me as a point of reference, to stay in control of the narrow distinction between reality and dreams. I worried they might not realize I was aware of their presence, and might think they didn't need to be with me, but I had no way of communicating with them.

Everyone seemed reluctant to leave the room, but John assured them that everything would be all right. "He'll still be here when you return," John said. "You're bringing my sandwich, so you had better hurry!"

When everyone had left the room, John searched for the right words. "Well, here we are. They're all gone now. You can quit pretending. Man, what gives you the right to disrupt everyone's life, anyway?"

Again my concentration failed.

*In a field behind the West Gardiner Grange Hall, the neighborhood kids are playing a championship wiffleball game, and everyone has come to watch. My brother is standing on second base wearing a cowboy outfit. The pitch is thrown to me at the plate, and I see the ball perfectly. It seems to be approaching in slow motion. I look like Willie Mays when I swing, but the ball smacks the catcher's mitt, and I strike out, losing the game.*

"Does he have any allergies?" an unknown voice that I assume to be a doctor asked.

24

"No, he never has had any in the past," Mom said.

"Have you noted anything out of the ordinary lately?" the voice asked.

"No," Mom said.

"I'm not sure he's been eating too well," John said. "He was telling me last week that he hasn't had much money for food."

*No, I've been eating well,* I thought.

"He has been eating quite a lot of macaroni and cheese, but I can't see where his diet is the problem," Lisa said.

"Has he been getting enough sleep?" the voice asked.

I tried to smile. *That guy doesn't know me.*

"I've never known him to skimp on sleep," Lisa said. "He was working sixty hours a week this summer, but he was doing OK."

"I noticed him being a little tired," my father said. "I told him to take care of himself, but Mark doesn't listen very well."

"He can be pretty stubborn," Lisa agreed.

"What's Mark been doing the last couple of weeks?" the unknown voice asked.

"Lisa is probably the most familiar with that," my father said. "What do you say, Lisa?"

"Well, I don't know where you want me to start, but I'll begin after he finished work at U-Haul this summer," Lisa said. "I know he went to a bachelor party on Cape Cod with some friends the next weekend. I was in Toronto that weekend."

"Cape Cod," the voice said. "That's interesting. Go on."

"The next weekend he and I went canoeing on the Saco River in Maine."

"Tell me about that. Did he drink the water?" the voice asked. "Were there a lot of mosquitoes?"

"The Saco is very clean where we were canoeing," Lisa said. "The water level was quite low. We would set up camp on the banks of the river, and always boiled the water or used water purification tablets."

"I bet he picked up something there," Mom said.

*No, no,* I disagreed silently.

"How were the mosquitoes?" the voice asked again.

"Not bad at all," Lisa said.

"But they were horrible at Small Point the next weekend," Suellen said.

"Mark and Lisa went camping with Suellen and me that next weekend down along the coast, at Hermit Island in Maine," John said.

"They were really thick," Lisa agreed. "We got eaten alive."

I did not want to listen anymore. I was tired of concentrating on the conversation and did not fight to stay alert as I drifted into my own world, recalling the night at Small Point.

*There are too many stars to count in the night sky, and in the distance, waves lap against the beach. Spruce trees protect me from the salt breeze, their sharp points silhouetted against the cobalt sky. Coals glisten as the fire burns out, and Lisa's warm hand slips into mine.*

"And then we went to Thailand," I heard Lisa say sometime later that afternoon. Much time had elapsed, because I could no longer feel the warmth of the sunlight shining through the window.

"What was Thailand like?" the unknown voice asked.

"It's hard to lump it all together. It was very different."

"What did you do there?"

"We spent a couple of weeks living in a bungalow on the beach off Ko Samui, an island off the east coast," Lisa said. "Then we went to see elephants…"

*Gray elephants dance across the marine blue water. The sky looks as harmless as a robin's egg, without clouds, and non-threatening. A bright glow makes the image sparkle.*

Dancing elephants. That was the last thing I remembered.

# Chapter 3

# The Coma

**"M**ark!" he shouted.

Frustration and passion rang in his voice. John believed he could reach me. At least he was not afraid of trying, and he felt a strong responsibility to try. Doctors had limitations, and John knew he could help. From talking with others months later, I pieced together some of the events during the weeks of my coma.

"Mark! Hang in there! Come on, Mark! You can't quit now, damn it!" I could feel him trying to will me back to consciousness, back to his world. "Fight it, Mark! Fight it! You can do it!"

It was the second day after my lapse into the coma. My family watched my corpse-like body, unresponsive and pale, lying on the bed. I was still alive, but no one knew for how long. My family had spent a sleepless night in the Intensive Care waiting room.

I was falling deeper and deeper into the coma, occasionally curling into the fetal position. I was no longer conscious of anything going on around me, but through my dream-state my mind was active and alive.

My unconscious self somehow heard John's message, and sensed the strength and resolve in the room. It would have been so easy, so peaceful to descend one more step. "I could come back," I told myself. The old wives' tale said that you never die in your dreams, and I can't disagree. My dreams continued.

*I do not understand the source of the chaos. I only know that I am frightened. I run. I run so fast that I soar three feet above the path, five feet, fifteen feet. I fly like a kite in March and peer down on the treetops below me. Anticipating my fall, I fear to look down any longer.*

On the third morning, Sam later told me he came to visit. He met Lisa in the hallway near the ICU nurses' station. She had spent the night awkwardly slumped in a waiting room chair, and was trying to rub the soreness out of her back and neck. Sam brought her a cup of coffee.

"So, how's he doing?" Sam asked. He saw me lying perfectly still; serene, even, if you didn't know my condition. Sam looked through the window into my room. He turned and shivered as he saw the respirator and an electroencephalograph.

"Not much change since I talked with you yesterday," Lisa said. "The doctors are worried about a possible infection."

A respiratory therapist went into my room, tying the cords of a surgical mask behind her head.

"How are you doing?" Sam asked Lisa. "You can't keep this up forever, you know."

"I know." Lisa's face was pale and troubled. "I'm not sure what I'm going to do. I can't go back to school and just leave Mark here."

Sam looked through the window into my room and watched the respiratory therapist as he talked with Lisa. He saw the therapist force a tube down my throat, shocking my body into a violent rage, as if electric currents were passing through it. My body jumped from the bed, coughing and thrashing spastically. Lisa followed Sam's eyes. She had seen this reaction several times before, so was unconcerned.

"Right now, I think I'll take this semester—" Lisa stopped talking as she saw Sam's face turn ashen.

Sam leaned his six-foot-three-inch frame against the wall. It was probably the smell of the antiseptics made him lightheaded, and he broke into a sweat. What if he'd caught what I had? We'd spent a lot of time together lately. Sam's eyes rolled back into his head as he silently slid down the wall into a limp heap on the floor.

I was no longer the center of attention. One nurse grabbed a nearby wheelchair, one quickly reached into a drawer for the smelling salts, and the smartest one held Sam. With the nurse waving the smelling salts under his nose, Sam quickly regained consciousness. Embarrassed but nervous, Sam consented to be wheeled to the emergency room for a precautionary check. His knees rose awkwardly high in the wheelchair as the nurse whisked him off. The diagnosis: nerves.

"Mr. and Mrs. Hathaway, I would like to talk with you, if I could."

"Certainly, Doctor. What is it?"

"I'm afraid it isn't very good news, but there is always hope," the doctor said. "We've determined that Mark has viral encephalitis. We are now trying to determine what strain he has."

My parents were not expecting good news, but somehow they had been hoping that someone would say my condition was improving. They appreciated the doctor's frankness and remained calm, on the surface. My mother later told me her reaction to the conversation with the doctors. She thought that a glimmer of hope was a start. She told me that she wondered whether I would survive for only the briefest moment, but rid herself of that unthinkable possibility. He will make it, she told herself.

"What can be done for him, Doctor?" my father asked.

"There isn't much that can be done," the doctor said. "It's mostly up to Mark at this point. All we can do is try to keep him alive. The worrisome thing about comas is that complications arise very quickly, and it's the complications that cause the most problems."

"What exactly is viral encephalitis?" Dad asked.

"It's a fairly general term indicating swelling of the brain," replied the doctor. "Not that much is known about encephalitis. As the name implies, Mark has a virus, and being a virus, doctors have little knowledge about it. There just isn't much we can do; antibiotics don't effectively fight viruses. The most common carriers of encephalitis are insects, usually mosquitoes, although there are many viruses which may cause the disease."

"A mosquito," my father repeated incredulously.

Therapy started. Once a patient loses his range of motion, the process of regaining it is very painful if possible at all. Therapy was also useful in stimulating my circulation and preventing bed sores.

By the end of the second week, the doctors grew increasingly silent, knowing that with each passing day, the probability of my survival lessened considerably. A routine developed. Adjusting to the new surroundings admirably, my mother got a part-time position at Northwestern.

Perhaps her major contribution was that she provided support for Lisa, and in her own way, Lisa provided support for my mother. Without knowing it, Lisa and my mother worked as a team. Each gave to the team unselfishly. Lisa gave youth, energy, and passion while my mother gave leadership, experience, and courage. Most importantly, they both gave unrelenting heart and faith. They were never ready to quit, and they fought so hard that no one else allowed themselves to quit either. If a coach had to select a team, he could not have chosen a better one. Both had the one trait that a good coach knows is irreplaceable: the will and the heart to win.

Each morning, Lisa would read the newspaper aloud to me, knowing that at times people in a comatose state can hear. She would read the sports page, not because she liked to read that section of the paper, but because she knew that sports was the section that I liked best. Lisa played the radio for me and talked in a normal voice as if I could respond. An unknowing observer might have thought she was a possessed woman. Lisa believed.

As the third week passed, doctors grew still more reserved as they were confronted by their own helplessness. Complications developed. I was plagued by a severe case of pneumonia, despite attempts by respiratory therapists to clear my lungs. Lesions were appearing on my skin, and I was losing weight much too rapidly.

Lisa said later that she watched my face deteriorate to the point that it appeared almost frightening, so pale, blank and sullen. She had caressed it often, traveling its contours with her warm, sensitive fingers. She did have doubts, but not about my ability to survive. She asked herself if I would have come to her side like she did mine. She wondered whether or not she should just go on living her own life and not concern herself with my situation so much. In her heart and soul she knew that she was doing the right thing. It didn't matter what anyone thought, it didn't even matter what I thought she decided. The right thing to do in situations like this is usually the hardest, she reasoned, and was determined to stay beside me for as long as it took. Lisa later told me how lonely she felt. She was not getting along well with her own family, and her best friend was lying comatose. Her close female friends were in Canada; although they tried to imagine her situation, they could never understand. She wanted to be held, and longed for someone to tell her that everything would return to normal. Lisa's life was changing forever. She was hesitant and frightened to be left alone.

The doctors grew even less encouraging. They did not want my family to have unrealistic expectations that were sure to be disappointed. The nurses were not discouraged; neither were the interns who were with me every day, all day. Even on days when they felt doubt, they did not show it. Many were the same age as me, and they took a personal interest in my case. They saw themselves lying in that bed, already looking half like a corpse. The nurses and interns related to Lisa and thought that if they were lying in my place, they would want their own version of Lisa sitting beside them. They were all determined to do what they could for me. I later learned that the nurses let Lisa eat the meals that were meant for me.

During the fourth week, the doctors decided that I should be moved from Intensive Care to another unit of the hospital. There was nothing further the doctors could do in ICU, and I was moved to a bed in the Infectious Disease Unit. I would still have a private room, and one wall of my room would have a window running the length of it, overlooking the nurses' station. The beds in ICU were needed for patients who required more immediate care.

"I'm sorry, Mrs. Hathaway, there just isn't much more we can do," the doctors told my mother. In private, however, I think that even they were beginning to believe I had a chance. With guarded optimism, they saw hope. Dr. Stand, my primary doctor and a religious man, showed his faith by suggesting that his prayer group pray for my recovery. He could not help but to be influenced by the people around me including Lisa, Mom and Dean Wilson.

Dr. Martin was the intern in charge of my case. He was a compassionate and capable doctor, and he spent long hours trying to unlock the mystery of my illness. Dr. Martin worked closely with my family, and always offered hope. "Mark can do it," he told them. "He's young and basically healthy." Each morning, Dr. Martin saw Lisa come into the hospital. He was amazed to see that her eyes still sparkled.

In the fifth week, my eyes opened. Nurses waved their hands in front of my face, but I stared directly ahead, my eyes not following movement and I did not see them. The first day my eyes stayed open for an hour.

The second day they remained open nearly twice as long. By the third day, nurses had to administer drops so that my eyes remained moist. My eyes closed periodically during the day, possibly as I slept. Anticipation grew as my eyes opened longer each day, but they still did not follow movement.

Meanwhile, my body was growing visibly weaker. My face was pale and sunken. I had jowls worse than those of former President Nixon, thin and chalky. The race was on. Would I wake before my body grew too weak to support life?

I could almost sense the tension during the sixth week. My pneumonia was worsening. Uncontrollable coughing fits ravaged my body. My skin grew dry and flaky, and a serious infection blocked my ear.

I can only imagine Lisa's emotions must have been drained. The previous six weeks had been a crash course in independent survival. Never again, she said, would she leave herself in such a vulnerable position, so heavily dependent on another person. She told me that she sat by my bedside and remembered our stays in Hong Kong.

Victoria Peak, overlooking the harbor, had been our favorite spot. We would grab a bottle of wine, flee the exotic smells and swarms of people, and catch the tram to the peak. The ride began in the city, where laundry hung from every window. The tram climbed past high-rise apartment buildings with rooftop swimming pools and tennis courts, and the ride ended in the land of Jaguars and Rolls Royces.

From there we'd walk uphill as the orange sun lowered in the sky. By the time we reached our secluded rock and opened the wine, neon lights lit the bustling city below. Red China, with all its mysteries, lay on the horizon directly in front of us, and cargo ships from around the world anchored on the outskirts of the harbor. We snuggled closer together when an ocean breeze cooled the land. As the sunset changed from yellow-orange to purple, the city lights twinkled, and we were gazing down at the strangest, loveliest city in the world.

During my comatose period, my body lay still, but my mind was active and alive. I was dreaming, a state not well understood. In *The Forgotten Dreams*, Erich Fromm calls dreams a "language in which inner experiences, feelings, and thoughts are expressed as if they were sensory experiences, events in the outer world." Sir Peter Medawar, a Nobel laureate, disagrees: "[T]he content of dreams may be totally devoid of meaning…dreams may be assemblages of thought elements that convey no information whatsoever." Did my dreams convey inner feelings or were they simply meaningless, random images?

My dreams during my comatose state fell into no easy categories. They were not all nightmares, nor were they all soothing. Whether I was being captured in Afghanistan, flown to a MASH unit in Korea for an operation, or burying supplies for the long winter ahead, the common thread—if one existed—was survival. I generally did not recognize the location or the time period of my dreams, and I could not explain the appearance of certain individuals.

Only one dream recurred regularly. In that dream, Lisa came from Montreal to visit. In one segment of that dream, I was released from the hospital, but I had to return periodically for checkups. Toward the end of each segment, I was extremely tired. Because this dream seemed so lifelike, it was not until Christmas, approximately six weeks after my eyes began to follow movement, that I realized my dream was, in fact, just that, and that I was still in the hospital.

One peculiarity of my dreams during my comatose period is simply that I remember so many of them. Some I can still recall at any time, while others flash into my mind at the oddest moments—during a meal or while watching a football game on television. I have already forgotten the dreams I had last night, but when those coma dream flashbacks occur, I am mesmerized, not only by the vision in my mind, but by the odd sensation of displacement that only dreams can evoke. It's hard for me to make sense or write about several of my most complex dreams.

# Chapter 4

# Awakening

It was night, and I could hear an Indian chanting. I felt hands beating on my chest, and realized that the Indian was chanting to the rhythm of those beats. I opened my eyes to see the Indian's profile with its sharp nose, and a tall feather silhouetted against an eerie glow. Closer examination revealed that the glow was cast by an electric night light over my bed.

My bed had been raised to a thirty-degree angle, giving me a surrealistically slanted perspective. Although I could not move, the angle afforded me a partial view of my surroundings. A window seemed to run the length of the right wall, but the Venetian blinds did not allow me to see what lay on the other side. They only let a slim edge of light into the room, which added to the eerie glow. A TV mounted on the wall opposite my bed provided a sharp contrast to the whiteness of the room: white walls and ceiling, white sheets, a white porcelain sink in the corner. The white sink had a modern chrome faucet that rose into a semicircle a foot above the porcelain.

The odor reminded me of a hospital visit to my grandfather when I was a small boy. The nurses had said I was too young, but they let me in because my grandfather had recently suffered a heart attack, and they were not sure I would get the opportunity to see him again. The air was stale and smelled of sickness and medicine. Feeling dizzy and queasy, I slumped to the floor in a faint. The nurses revived me with smelling salts, and everyone had a good laugh.

Now, as my eyes peered from my raised bed, I imagined myself in my grandfather's hospital bed. *Was I now that pale body, with a forlorn look on my face?*

The beating and chanting continued. I looked more closely at the other person in the room. His flowing black hair was gathered into a braid that disappeared down his back. I wondered about the black framed glasses he was wearing. *Did Indians wear glasses?* My childhood vision of Indian warriors consisted of half-naked savages who shot bows and arrows and rode ponies bareback. Of course, that was an out-of-date picture, but *why was he chanting?* He was even wearing an Indian headband with a single feather sticking straight up from the back of his head. He wore turquoise and coral jewelry, much like the Tibetan refugees I had seen in the mountains of Nepal.

What puzzled me most were his modern clothes, covered by a light blue medical jacket. On the jacket a dark blue lapel pin read, "Billy Feathers, Respiratory Therapist."

*Where am I NOW?* I wondered. *Is this really happening? Am I in a dream? Am I living my life in a Salvador Dali painting?*

Billy Feathers soon stopped beating and chanting. I felt as if I was in a dentist chair as he fed a quarter-inch plastic tube into my mouth. I heard the hissing sound of air passing through the tube as he forced it deeper into my throat.

"Here you go," he said. "Take a little of this. This will help you clear your lungs."

Violent coughs wracked my body. Life seemed to stand still as I gagged and searched for something to hold on to, but I could not control the movement. My body was zapped of all its strength, and I thankfully re-entered a world of peace.

I awoke to find myself peering through metal bars into a private bathroom not more than five feet away. It was early morning; I guessed five thirty or six. I was lying on my side, but the bed appeared to be at the same thirty-degree angle it had been before. The bars were preventing me from falling to the floor. My neck was tilted in an awkward position, and my nose was pressed into the bars. I wanted to roll onto my back, but my body would not respond. Someone was behind me, trying to tie a ribbon behind my neck.

"Now be patient, and this won't take long," a woman said in a cheerful voice. Being awakened at five thirty in the morning with my nose pressed against metal bars, I was not equally cheerful. The sound of her voice frustrated me. *Can't she see I'm uncomfortable, and why can't I move or talk? Why is she in such a good mood?* The woman talked as if she were alone in the room. She seemed to be talking more to keep herself company than to carry on a conversation with me.

She pulled the ribbon tightly around my neck. It seemed to be attached to a plastic tube implanted in my throat. The woman untied the ribbon, and cut another length. She meticulously threaded the ribbon through a slot on one side of the plastic tube, and laboriously attempted to do the same to the other side without success. I could hear her cheery voice in the background as I strained with impatience. I no longer paid close attention to her words because I knew that what she was saying was not meant for me.

Finally, she pulled the ribbon through the slot, and remained cheerful as she pulled the ribbon tighter and tighter. As the woman tightened the ribbon, it became more difficult to breathe. I tried to speak, but I could not utter a sound. At last, she loosened the ribbon and tied it into a knot at the back of my neck. As she tidied the bedside, her smile revealed that she was satisfied with a job well done.

The woman looked like a waitress as I imagined they had looked in the forties. She was in her mid-fifties with a dark complexion. Her jet black hair was covered by a hairnet like the ones I had seen only a few older waitresses wearing in diners back home. Perched on her hairnet was a white nurse's cap. She was far removed from the young nurses I had known.

*Have I gone back in time?* I wondered. *Why is this plastic tube in my throat, anyway?* With the questions left unanswered, I drifted into yet another world.

I woke as the tourniquet pinched the hairs on my arm. It reminded me of my days teaching English in Taiwan. One of my students had pinched the blond hairs on my arm in curiosity. He was intrigued, as Chinese have little or no body hair. He giggled as I turned, and his mind drifted back to the English class. To make sure he stayed focused, I asked him a question in English.

The tourniquet was made of elastic tubing approximately one inch wide. The elastic gripped my arm snugly. In Boy Scouts, I had learned that a tourniquet was a last resort to stop bleeding because it could cause loss of limb. I knew I was not bleeding, and did not know the reason for the tourniquet.

A woman held a large syringe up to the light. She looked sinister, and did not realize I was watching her. The syringe was filled with oxygen, and my heart skipped a beat as I realized I would die if she injected me with air. I could not shut my eyes, but could only stare directly ahead. I felt the prick of the needle piercing my skin, but nothing happened. She tried again, and I could still feel the pressure of the tourniquet on my arm as she left the room. I was alone and could not speak or move. Panicking, I shut my eyes and did not open them again until she returned. I looked at my arm and felt relieved to see it there, and then it all became clear to me. The woman was only extracting a sample of my blood.

The prick of a safety pin startled me. Five faces with blue coats surrounded my bed. As before, the bed was tilted at a thirty-degree angle, affording me a limited view of the white room that had become my temporary home. Each of the five wore a dark blue pin on his left lapel. Each pin bore a name and the word "Intern," except for one pin that read "Resident" after the name.

The resident talked as the others listened with curiosity. He looked slightly older than the others, and seemed to be trying to impress the four with his knowledge. One after another, each intern followed the resident's lead, and curiously pricked me with their pins, fascinated by the fact that I showed no outward reaction.

*Damn, what do they think I am, anyway, a human pin cushion? Don't they realize I can feel those pin pricks, and they hurt like hell?* I was growing accustomed to watching my own body as if I were a stranger living in another shell. I was beginning to understand that for some unknown reason, I was unable to move or to speak. I wanted to tell the interns to go away, or to at least have some respect for my body; I was not a human pincushion. I had no great desire to escape my world.

With the same fascination, they each took turns rubbing the bottom of my feet with a reflex hammer. Again, no reaction.

"As you can see, he has lost the reflex actions," the resident said. "Chances are very slim that he will ever regain them. I personally don't expect him to live much longer." The medical students did not realize I could see them, much less understand what they were saying.

I later learned that my eyes had been open for more than two weeks. When I awoke from my coma, I had Locked-in Syndrome, a condition in which the mind is alive and active, but the body does not move. I could

38

not control the link between my brain and any movement whatsoever. I had lost nearly all muscle strength and tone. On top of that, my eyes would close at times, but I could not control the blinks. I did move involuntarily. Sometimes my arms and legs thrashed spastically when respiratory therapists forced a suction tube down my throat. My fingers, for example, could be manipulated, but I could not control them. I could not send a message from my brain to my fingers to move as I wanted.

As the resident lifted my leaden right arm and bent it at the elbow, he said, "He has lost much of his range of motion. If he does live—and again, I don't think he will—you can see that he will have only limited use of his right arm."

His words made little sense to me. For the moment, I was content lying in the world with the surrealistic slant. I was not sure why, but I felt glad to be alive. Time assumed a new meaning; a month seemed like a long time, two months seemed an eternity. Moving or speaking had little importance, but I did want to see my family.

I thought more about the resident's words. He had intruded upon my tranquil world, presenting ideas with which I did not want to concern myself. *He has a right to his opinion*, I thought. *I was not threatened.*

People had intruded on my world before. As a tenth grader at Phillips Exeter Academy in New Hampshire, I had dealt with another authoritarian figure who had entered my world and acted as though he knew the answer—the one and only answer for me. The pressure on a fifteen-year-old boy from a small Maine town to conform was overwhelming. My Spanish teacher had wanted to mold me into agreeing with his way of doing things. He did not like me, and did not care how difficult my Maine accent made it to distinguish the "R" sound and thus hear the Spanish sounds. He made me feel inadequate, and wanted to prevent my going to Spain for study the following school year. Another Spanish teacher had come to my rescue.

After I returned from Spain, my friends had urged me to confront the first teacher, because I had received an 800 (the highest score possible) on my Spanish achievement test. I had no interest in doing so.

What the teacher thought had not been important to me then, and what the resident thought was not important to me now. They were only hurdles in my path. What was important in both instances was what I thought was possible. I would not be persuaded by individuals I did not respect.

For the present, my world consisted of that bed at a thirty-degree angle in that white room. It was not important to me to move my arm or regain my reflex actions, or even to "live" as the resident defined it. I was content to lead the life I was living, and I wanted to see my family.

"Mark, are you awake this morning?" a male voice asked. "Ah, I see you are. Good morning, and welcome back."

I looked up to see a bearded face with glasses. He was talking as though I had been on a long journey. Although this official-looking man appeared to be only in his mid-thirties, his light hair was already thinning. On his white medical jacket, a multicolored pin read, "Smoking Stinks," and sticking out of its pocket, I could see the earpieces of a stethoscope.

*Welcome back? What did that mean?*

I was sure I had seen this man before. I tried to place his face. Could he be the image of the Picasso painting I had seen somewhere earlier? This time his eyes were lined up normally, and his head did not appear enlarged or distorted.

"Remember me?" he asked. "I'm Dr. Stand. I met you some time ago in the emergency room."

He shined a small medical flashlight into my eyes, and asked me to look first to one side, then to the other. I was hoping to get a response, some signal of his expectations, but he remained silent. I felt comfortable and confident that I was in capable hands. He inspected my ear, and found that I had developed an infection.

He placed warm fingers on my feet. They were smooth and uncallused, like a dentist's hands. "Now," he said, "I want to see you wiggle your toes."

The bed remained at a thirty-degree angle, enabling me to see my toes. Although I could sense hot and cold and the pressure of his hands, I could not understand how my toes were connected to the rest of my body.

"Come on," he said. "Move your toes. Aw, come on. You're not trying hard enough."

Damn him. I could not try any harder. With all my energy, I strained to move them, but my toes would not budge. I searched my mind for the connection to my toes.

"You can do it. Come on, wiggle your toes."

I stared at my toes, hoping that if I fixated on them, the connection between my mind and my feet would emerge. I strained to move, but watched in frustration as my toes remained like those of a stone statue. I had exhausted my energy supply, and failed to move them even a millimeter. I was too tired to deal with my failure. I just wanted to escape and leave my frustrations behind me.

"Oh, hi! I'm Marilyn, your favorite nurse." Her face was only a foot away from my nose. I guessed her age to be about twenty-three. Attractive and friendly looking, her brown hair dropped to the shoulders of her green surgical scrubs.

*What did she say?* It took me a moment to place her in the same environment as the white room. *Is this chick serious?*

"What are you doing to the poor guy?" another nurse asked from across the room.

"I'm just teaching him early, so that he always knows his favorite nurse," Marilyn said with a laugh.

"Oh, sure," the other nurse nodded. "You get first dibs. You just wait."

"He'll always know who he can rely on when he needs protection from you clumsy guys," Marilyn said. She turned back to me. "Seriously, I'm Marilyn, your primary nurse, and this is Debbie." Then she purposely whispered loudly so that Debbie could overhear, "You'd better learn to stay away from her if you want to be safe."

"Oh, cut it out. He's going to have a horrible first impression of me." Debbie put one hand to her mouth and leaned toward me. "Don't listen to a word she says. She's even nuttier than she appears." Debbie was also about twenty-three, pretty, with a nice smile. I immediately liked the two nurses; their constant chatter would keep me entertained.

"Dr. Stand wanted us to rig this special buzzer," Marilyn said. "Whenever you want help, push this, and a light will go on at the nurses' station. It may be hard for you to operate at first, but you'll learn. We'll put it right by your head so that all you have to do is shift your weight a little."

I wanted to nod to show them I understood, but they had to assume that I did. I was grateful that they acted as if I understood. As the nurses went on to other duties, I drifted back to sleep.

I woke again to the sound of friendly voices. It was my friend Sam, talking with my mother. Dark beard and hair on top of a six-foot-three-inch frame made my friend easy to recognize. I'd always chuckled when

I asked why girls went after the tall, dark, and handsome types like Sam, but secretly I wondered why I always reminded them of their brother or best friend. Sam and I had become good friends during our first days at Northwestern. Although he was from Illinois, he had gone to college at Bowdoin in Maine, and many of his relatives lived in Hallowell, a small town near Gardiner. Knowing that he was familiar with my home territory made me feel comfortable with him, and a camaraderie developed. I could not believe that Sam was talking and joking with my mother as though he knew her well.

*What is my mother doing here? What is this, another one of my dreams? She is supposed to be in Maine. Aren't I in Evanston?*

"I brought you a little present, something to give you an incentive to get better. The doctors say your eyes are starting to follow movement. Welcome back. Did you have a good sleep?" Sam chuckled.

*Where have I been? Why is everyone welcoming me back as though I went on some trip or something?*

"I know studying is no fun," Sam continued, "but don't you think you reacted a bit too much? Do you want me to open this for you?"

I was glad he did not wait for an answer, and I was relieved to see people who made me feel comfortable. They talked to me in a relaxed tone, as if I understood every word they were saying—not like my father, who still shouts into the telephone receiver because he does not trust that the people on the other end of the line can hear him. It seemed they had known all along what others had not: that behind my eyes I had been traveling on an odyssey, and that I would soon be well and rejoin them.

Sam took the wrapping paper off the present, revealing a rolled-up poster. With care, he began to unroll it. "We're going to tape this to the ceiling." His smile showed that he was enjoying this present as much as I was. I stared with fascination and pleasure as he showed me the poster with a laugh. At the bottom it read, "Miss June. Playmate of the Year."

I listened intently as Sam and my mother discussed how graduate school was going for Sam. He told me that I was probably better off where I was because the workload was becoming unbearable. I could tell that my mother enjoyed his company. In a world where I could offer no communication, fresh, sharp minds were welcome.

"Let's see, what else should you know? It's been a cool autumn, you really haven't missed much. The Phillies won the Series, and can you believe it? Ronald Reagan is the new President!"

## Chapter 5

# The Ultimate Journey

**"H**ello, Mark!" A familiar voice woke me from my dream. Lisa was beaming in the doorway, looking anxious to discover what truths lay ahead. She moved slowly, laughing nervously as she conversed with my mother and Sam. Her eyes searched for movement from my still body, but she saw none, except for my eyes following her every move. As she drew near the bed, my mother and Sam left the room to give us some time alone.

The excitement in her face showed the vitality I wanted to capture. Her bright blue eyes filled with tears as our eyes met. My face stayed expressionless, but I have no doubt my eyes reflected her own hope and triumph.

"I knew you would do it if anyone could." She laughed through her tears. "You really had us going there for a bit. You always did have a sense for the dramatic." Lisa's tears were tears of joy. She picked up my hand from the bed and held it. Warmth and energy flowed through her hand, and I could feel its contours.

For the first time I was excited about getting well. I longed to embrace and comfort her.

"You don't have to worry now, I'll be here as much as possible," she told me. "You know, they try to kick me out of here at nine o'clock." Lisa searched for acknowledgement. She had lingering doubts she later told me—not about my mind, but about whether I appreciated her presence.

"Just squeeze my hand if everything is all right," she said, squeezing my hand. "I need to feel your hand. I need to know that you still love me."

I wanted to give her that response. I loved Lisa more than ever. I did not know what had transpired since we had last talked by telephone on a Sunday night in late September. I felt different, but I did not know why, and I didn't know that weeks had passed since the last time we'd talked. I had seen her in my dreams. My coma dreams had seemed very real, and at that point I believed that my dreams had actually occurred.

"Please give me some sign, Mark."

I wanted to squeeze. I tried and tried to muster the energy to squeeze her hand, to give her even the slightest response. I did not understand what was happening; I could only sense that Lisa needed my reassurance. I wanted to grunt and groan and strain. I did not even know how to focus my energy to try. More than anything else in the world, I wanted to reach out to her and squeeze, but I could not.

Something serious had happened to me, but I did not know what it was. From the surroundings, it seemed obvious that I was in the hospital, but I was not even sure of that. I felt odd. I had lost twenty-five pounds and was unable to move, even to blink my eyes. I was conscious and aware, but a haze of unreality lurked on the periphery. I searched for the connection between my mind and my body.

I was locked in.

If anything seemed real to me, it was television. I could focus on a limited space and exclude outside stimuli that I did not comprehend. Television was a link to the past. I could forget not being able to speak or move. I could live in my mind, with television providing the environment. Worlds would change rapidly with each program, with each commercial.

The world of Captain Kirk and Mr. Spock mesmerized me, especially when the Enterprise was traveling about the galaxy. For a brief moment I was there, infinity to my right and left. I was floating as though walking in space. I would not fall, but I dared not look down. Captain Kirk enjoyed the challenges he faced with the crew of the Enterprise, and somehow he always managed the crisis well. He always maintained his poise, and was confident that if a solution to his predicament existed, he would find it. With Captain Kirk at my side, I was optimistic that we would discover a solution to my predicament.

The doctors did not share my optimism. They had no miracle drug, and they honestly did not know what the outcome of my illness would be. I heard constant talk that I could plateau; my progress could stop at any moment.

I liked the odds. I was alive. No one said that I could not recover, and I forged ahead, not looking behind me. Lisa, my mother, and I were all confident that if I did hit a plateau, we could handle it.

Sometimes I lost my sense of reality when nurses turned me on my side to prevent bedsores. My head would spin, and I would close my eyes to control the spinning. When I opened them again, my mind would drift to places like Nepal. During those spells, I relived my past.

The Nepalese skies of February were as blue as Lisa's eyes. Snow-covered mountains rose from each side of the valley in which my sister, my friend Dana and I were trekking. On the ancient stone trail to Muktenath, we passed a pilgrim turning his prayer wheel, one for each psalm he mumbled. He did not acknowledge us as he walked in a trance, lost in his own world. We hiked into a cold, damp rhododendron forest. I imagined what the forest would look like when the buds sprang to life in a month. I turned as I heard a branch snap.

"Look, a monkey!" I whispered. The white monkey with a black mask was joined by more monkeys, hundreds of snowy monkeys wearing black masks. They seemed oblivious to our presence as they swung from branch to branch. We stood frozen in awe. As suddenly as the monkeys appeared, they disappeared into the dark forest.

At other times, I would stare at a snapshot of my sister's baby son, nicknamed Bubs. I did not believe that my sister Nancy could have produced a chubby baby like Bubs. In his Jolly Jumper, he reminded me of Buddha smiling on his throne. He looked as if he were the only one who knew where to find the key that would unlock the mystery of life.

I had read an account of the life of Buddha, who had lived in India more than two thousand years ago. By concentrating on the sound of a river, he heard the sounds of life, the agony, the pleasure of it all. If I listened intently, maybe I could hear the sounds of life in the humming of the fluorescent lights. Anything, I thought, would be better than my aches and pains.

Golf had been one of my favorite pastimes. People like to say that golf is ninety-nine percent mental. If that's true, my golf game was spectacular. My physical game was lacking, but that was a tiny part of the whole. I was good in my locked-in fantasy. I played in an imaginary final threesome at the Masters with Jack Nicklaus and Arnold Palmer. Jack was not a problem, but Arnie beat me on the 18th hole when he sank a twenty-foot birdie putt.

I looked forward to therapy for the simple reason that my body would be moved, and my aches temporarily relieved. Susan was my physical therapist when I first woke from the coma. She would stretch my legs for me, as I was unable to do so. Not only were my muscles extremely weak, I could not forge a link between my brain and various muscles in my body. I could not send the message that would make my fingers squeeze Lisa's hand. With Susan's encouragement, I was beginning to understand that link.

While physical therapy concentrated on my legs, occupational therapy centered on my arms and fingers. In those first days, I did not like my occupational therapist, Arlene. She made me work too hard, and I disdained the exercises Arlene had me do. I was a poor patient. Furthermore, she constantly chit-chatted with my mother while she was doing exercises with me. Jokes rolled off her tongue. Arlene had an excellent sense of humor, but each time I started to laugh, my sides ached and I would cough. The harder I tried not to laugh, the more I coughed. Without fail, I would cough until I vomited, but because vomiting was not unusual for me, Arlene never understood why I was not fond of her during those first days.

My speech therapist, Jean, first tried to teach me to signal "yes" or "no" by blinking. One blink would mean "yes" and two blinks would mean "no." For days, I tried to control the movement in my eyelids, without much success. It was nearly two weeks from the time I first awoke until I was able to control the blinks of my eyes and signal "yes" or "no."

Meanwhile, Lisa was attempting to teach me to shake my head "yes" or "no." She tried to convince Jean that the half hour each day would be better spent training me to shake my head, rather than wasted on trying to get me to blink. I tried to nod in agreement, and one day I succeeded. At about the same time I learned to blink. The headshake was barely noticeable, but it was more reliable than blinking.

Jean moved on to flashcards to test my cognitive reasoning. She would hold up a blue card.

"Is this red?" she would ask. "Is this green?"

I would shake my head. "No."

"Is this blue?" she asked.

I often shook my head "no" again. I did not want to play this silly, demeaning game. I was frustrated. Of course, I knew the answer to her questions. The inability to voice my frustrations made me sulk like a child.

Another reason I answered negatively, although I knew the correct answer, was because I could not control my headshakes well. If I were concentrating on shaking my head "no" time and again, it was very difficult to change my thought process and signal "yes." Blinking might have been more reliable.

My ability to signal "yes" or "no" was an important stage in my development. It enabled me to communicate with Lisa and to play the game "Twenty Questions." The game often helped relieve my pain. Pain was almost constant, because my body ached from its inability to shift to a new position. "Twenty Questions" would pinpoint my pain and allow Lisa to move or massage the part of my body that was hurting. Often, however, the game ended in frustration.

If my neck hurt, as it often did, Lisa would ask, "OK, first, is the pain above your waist?"

"Yes," I would nod.

"Is the pain in your arms?"

"No." Shake.

"Is the pain in your shoulders?"

"No."

"OK, is it in your head?"

"No."

"No! Where is it, then?" she asked. "Is it your toes?"

Again I would shake, "No."

"OK, let's start over. Is it above the waist?" and the questions would continue.

Lisa and I both grew more frustrated with each "no." Her speed increased as she searched for the source of the pain. When she finally came to the neck, I often shook my head "no" again, increasing Lisa's bewilderment. It was the same problem I had with Jean in speech therapy. If I was in the sequence of shaking "no," changing my thought process to signal "yes" before Lisa moved to another part of my body was extremely difficult. Often I would signal "yes" after Lisa had moved on to another part of the body, adding to her confusion. Sometimes she had to leave before we pinpointed the source of my pain. When she left, I lay frustrated and in pain, waiting to be moved again.

Fanny was my private-duty nurse on the three-to-eleven shift. As a private-duty nurse, she had no other patients. A motherly black lady, she possessed certain appropriate physical attributes which gave her an endearing quality. Fanny came to work with a broad smile, always ready to challenge me.

"If you behave today, I might roll you over and let you look at that disgusting Playmate you have hanging on your door. You'd like that, wouldn't you?" She laughed, not expecting an answer. "You'll remind me to brush your teeth later, won't you?"

I hated to have my teeth brushed, and would try a symbolic resistance, but she knew I would eventually give in. I needed dental care. My teeth ground almost constantly. The sound was deafening, and I was worried that they would grind away.

When I saw Fanny coming after me with a toothbrush in her hand, my jaw automatically clenched, but I could not move far. Eventually, Fanny would overpower me and force her fingers into my mouth. *Can't I make my decisions for myself?* I thought. *Can't Fanny at least use toothpaste, instead of that disgusting stuff the hospital supplies?* The taste lingered in my mouth for hours.

Besides grinding teeth, my body was wracked by other involuntary movements. My head and body jerked uncontrollably to the side at any sudden noise. Grinding produced saliva, so I drooled incessantly. I was not an inspiring sight.

My mother later told me that she often ran into Fanny in the hospital cafeteria. "It's getting so I'm always thinking of Mark's health when I'm not on duty, Mrs. Hathaway," she said. "I don't sleep well, and that's not good."

"You're great with Mark, Fanny," Mom said. "I feel very secure when I know you are there with him. Of all the nurses, you get the most out of him."

One day not long after this conversation, Fanny called in sick. She often came to visit and monitor my progress after that, but never worked the three-to-eleven shift again. Everyone was disappointed to see her leave, and she was missed greatly. My mother told me that Fanny felt she was getting too involved in my case. I was sad because it was love and devotion like Fanny's that spurred me on.

Lisa and my mother entertained my visitors. I was the focal point of the visits, but I was not very sociable, unable to participate in a conversation. My abilities were limited to grinding my teeth, drooling and sweating. People came to marvel at the strength, energy and determination of the two women who were at my side. For whatever reason my friends came, I appreciated their visits, and they added fuel to my growing desire to get well.

My friend Dana flew to Chicago from St. Louis five times while I was in the hospital. I had known him since we were both four years old, when he and his twin brother used to chase me around our neighborhood with nail-studded boards. We had played sports together, built cabins, and sneaked into the woods to smoke our first cigarettes. After high school, I had convinced him to travel with me for six months to Spain, across Europe and Central Asia, and on to Nepal. Often the only two Westerners surrounded by foreign faces, we had learned to trust and depend upon one another.

Lisa's mother came from Toronto with a bright red poinsettia for my room. The visit was a much-needed relief for Lisa, and a chance for her to leave the hospital and explore Chicago.

Like my other visitors, Lisa's mother peered down at me. My blank expression told her that I did not realize all that was happening. As an occupational therapist, she knew the effects of encephalitis, from death to brain damage. "You'll be all right," she said. "Lisa assures me that you can pull through."

I also had regular visitors from the area, such as Sam and Dean Wilson. They brought gifts and stories about people I knew, but the most important gift was their humor.

"They tell me you used to play on the Jackson football team," Dean Wilson said. Jackson was a women's college at Tufts University, where I had spent my undergraduate years. "Wasn't that a little rough for you? I hear those Jackson girls are pretty tough to handle!" We wagered $5 on the outcome of the Tufts-Bates football game, my alma mater versus his. When we heard Tufts had won the game, I could lie smug, knowing that he would have to wait another year for a chance at revenge. If Bates had won, I would have had to suffer a lecture on the virtues of his alma mater.

Visitors were often disappointed by my facial expressions. They would try to make me smile by telling their funniest jokes, but a permanent scowl was etched on my face. Even when I felt happy, I frowned. Weak facial muscles kept me from smiling, and made my face sag.

Some of my favorite jokes were on the re-runs of *M*A*S*H*, which I watched every night. One night my mother watched as I reacted to each joke as it rolled off Hawkeye's tongue. Mom told me later that what impressed her most was the speed of my reactions. Until that night, she had watched fearfully, not knowing whether my mind was alert. At that point, she knew without a doubt that I was still capable of facing the challenges before me.

Lisa was the first person to see me smile. Word traveled rapidly throughout the unit, and I was bombarded with comedians. No one was satisfied with one smile. They did not realize that smiling on demand was not a simple task. I felt like a child forcing a "natural" smile for a family portrait.

Gardiner, Maine, where I was born and raised, is a quiet Maine town of 6,500. It is an old factory town; the factories are closed now, but the people manage to survive. Being isolated during the winter months brings a closeness to the community. Gardiner is not one of the coastal Maine villages that attract photographers, artists, and tourists, but it was always a stabilizing force in my background, and when my time came to leave it, the town gave me a solid support system. No matter where I was or what happened to me, I always relied on the world of Gardiner, Maine.

At the age of fourteen, I began to seek challenges beyond the protection of the imaginary walls of Gardiner. I embarked on my first journey, from Gardiner to Phillips Exeter Academy in New Hampshire. A new world of wealth, power, and prestige began to unfold. I was forced to question my own values. If I wanted to survive, I had to adapt.

At sixteen, I spent my junior year of high school in Barcelona, Spain, at that time a city of more than two million people. Living with a Spanish family, I experienced a new culture. Franco was in power, and I had difficulty accepting the restrictions he placed on the Spanish people. With naïve interest, I participated in an anti-Franco demonstration with both Spanish and American friends. They stopped to talk with other students; I walked on twenty yards ahead of them before I realized they had stopped. I turned to wait.

Riot police surprised me, prodding me with their billy clubs, and finally dragging me across the street to a waiting Jeep. I pretended to be an innocent tourist, and after a long body search, they let me go. Meanwhile, my friends notified authorities at the school I was attending and they, in turn, notified my Spanish family.

When I finally walked up the six flights of stairs to my host family's apartment, I had the biggest surprise of the day. My Spanish mother chased me back downstairs with a raised frying pan!

After graduating from Exeter, I began another journey. This time I traveled for six months from Spain overland through several countries including Italy, Bulgaria, Iran, Afghanistan, and India to Nepal. My friend Dana and I met my sister in Istanbul, and we journeyed together into lands that were in sharp contrast to Gardiner, Maine or Exeter, New Hampshire. For an eighteen-year-old, it was a great learning experience. Not only did I learn history and anthropology, I learned about independence and friendship. I returned to the States and enrolled at Tufts University in Boston.

Four years later, I set off once again, this time to the Far East and Southeast Asia. I worked in Taiwan and traveled to Hong Kong, China, Japan, Thailand, and the Philippines.

I came back to the States to enroll in Northwestern's Kellogg Graduate School of Management in Evanston, Illinois, where I fell into the coma. This journey I was now traveling was the longest of them all. I had voyaged to the edge of consciousness and beyond, down a road of mystery and dreams. Before reaching the end of that road, I had turned and started back. I had to remember all that I had learned. I had to remember the chess games with my brother, the challenge of leaving home for the first time, and all the lessons learned in places like Spain, Afghanistan, Nepal, and Japan.

My support systems were all there—my family, my friends, my hometown—but it was up to me alone to put those support systems to work. I would have the final say in my destiny. Never before had that been so clear to me.

With the turn of my head, with the single wiggle of my toe, with the slightest movement of my finger, I traveled further than I ever had before. This journey was the most exhilarating, the most risky, and presented the greatest challenges of all. The energy it took to wiggle my toes was greater than the energy it took to travel thousands of miles. I did not know my final destination, but I knew that I was on my ultimate journey.

# Chapter 6

# Suspended

"**O**kay, now how are we going to do this?" Marilyn, my primary nurse, raised her voice above the chatter. Six nurses were about to lift me from the hospital bed that had been my home for the past two months to a waiting cardiac chair. A cardiac chair is a cross between a reclining lounge chair and a wheelchair. It was a padded chair on three-inch wheels that would be my first step toward freedom and mobility. The chair would allow me to leave my room and return to the world beyond its walls.

The six nurses were nearly as excited as I was. They positioned themselves around my bed, three on each side. "Okay, everyone quiet down," Marilyn ordered.

"I hope you are not too scared, Mark," Debbie, another nurse, whispered. "We'll try not to drop you."

"No, we're old hands at this," Marilyn said. "Of course, the others were all ninety-pound little old ladies, and we only dropped two of them."

"Quiet!" she said. The laughing nurses tried to be serious, but inside they were bubbling with excitement.

Underlying my own anticipation was a tinge of anxious tension. I wanted the nurses to have a good time, but I wished they would remember that this was my fragile body they were lifting into the chair.

At the count of one, each of the nurses clutched an edge of the sheet that would be used for my transfer. The principle was simple; I would lie on the sheet while they lifted me into the chair. I wanted to give them all a last word of caution, but I still could not speak. *Here goes*, I thought. I worried about the ability of the three nurses on the right side of the bed to reach all the way across the bed to the waiting chair.

At the count of two, the nurses bent their knees and prepared themselves for the upcoming lift. It was too late to worry; I only prayed that all would go well. "Three!"

The sheet was uneven as the nurses lifted it toward the cardiac chair. I started to roll. As I feared, the nurses on the right side of my bed could not reach the chair with me on the sheet. I was rolling out of control. I wanted to grab hold of something, but I could not. I felt like an Eskimo being tossed into the air. I thought I would land safely, but I was not absolutely sure.

Luckily, the nurses managed to prevent me from rolling onto the floor. With nervous giggles, they reassured me.

"Sorry, Mark, we'll get it right this time!"

"Don't worry, we won't drop you."

This time two of the nurses rested one knee on the bed. I had confidence in them, but I held my breath until I glided into the chair.

Earlier that day, Dr. Stand had asked if I wanted to sit in a chair. I enthusiastically nodded "yes." Little did I realize the agony it would cause.

I was beginning to move my extremities, but my movement was limited. I could not move my arms with any precision. After the first five minutes in the chair, my arm started to slide on the vinyl armrest. I wanted to adjust it, but it would not respond. I tried again and again, but each time I failed. As my arm inched closer to the edge, I looked over at my mother knitting peacefully in the chair, but she did not notice my concern. I wanted someone to be as alarmed as I, but no one noticed.

Within seconds, my arm fell into my lap. I tried to rotate it, but again I was unsuccessful. My mother sat six feet away, and I had no method of communicating with her. For two hours I watched the second hand of the clock jump from one agonizing second to the next, my arm throbbing with pain. I stared at the clock, willing it to go more quickly. Come on, time. Come on!

When Marilyn asked, "Do you want to go back to bed?" I eagerly nodded "yes."

*Oh, please hurry, Marilyn*, I thought. *I promise to be a good kid. Remember, you're my favorite nurse!*

"Okay, in a few minutes. We'll get some nurses together."

The "few minutes" stretched into another half hour of pain as Marilyn gathered the six busy nurses. I never thought a hospital bed would be so inviting, but when the nurses finally transferred me back to bed, I breathed easier. Another mini-crisis was over.

"Everyone is coming for Thanksgiving. Nancy, Bill, and Bubs are coming from Rhode Island on their way to Atlanta. John and Suellen are coming from Baltimore. Suellen's pregnant, you know. Dad's coming out early," my mother said.

Knowing that my brother and sister were coming gave me another incentive to improve. I wanted to make my headshakes more reliable, and be able to shake hands to greet them. Thanksgiving came quickly, but I managed to make the communication improvements I wanted.

Bubs, my sister's baby, was the talk of the hospital. Everyone from doctors to cleaning ladies marveled at how chubby and good-natured he seemed. Nancy had planned this visit for weeks. She was eager for me to see the dramatic changes in him since August when we had walked in the park. Bubs was too young to visit my room, so the plan was to put me into the cardiac chair and wheel me to the elevator where he was waiting.

By now the nurses were familiar with the routine of my transfer, and cheerfully lifted my sheet into the chair as I held on for the ride. Two nurses wheeled me down the hallway. Halfway to the elevator, the excitement and the motion proved too much for my stomach; like a child riding in a car for the first time, I vomited profusely. Nancy sadly agreed that the one-hundred-yard trip was too much for me, and I was not able to see my nephew during his stay.

During this period, the pneumonia worsened, wracking my body with terrible coughs. Projectiles of phlegm would hit the television screen, suspended fifteen feet away.

My brother spent long hours shouting encouragement. "Come on, Mark. The more you cough, the quicker you clear your lungs and get better." John, who stood six-foot -three and weighed 210 pounds, wished that he could help me withstand the physical abuse. He could see that my body was drained of energy after each attack. In those moments when everything seemed to stop, I was happy to look up and see my brother standing beside me.

I was glad that I was the one bed-ridden. *So what if I can't start school this fall,* I thought. *I'll be back.* I could handle whatever happened. I was regaining control and confidence, and I knew that my situation would change. *Even if it doesn't change, I can handle it,* I thought. *What if this had happened to John? He has a wife to support and a baby on the way. This would be devastating to him.*

It could not have happened at a better time for me. If it had happened a week earlier, I would not have been insured, and I was sure the hospital bills were already astronomical. If it had happened a year earlier, I might have been on some remote island in the Philippines, and then what?

*What would it have been like if I had died? They would have had a funeral. For a couple of weeks, friends and relatives would have asked each other, "Did you hear what happened to Mark? He died, you know. Man, it was terrible he died so young. He had so many things ahead of him. Why did he go to the Philippines? Why did he take that risk?"*

*Damn,* I thought, *they're not going to say that about me.* They would go on living their own lives, and that was the way I guessed I would want it. But I did not think of myself as a memory, a dead end in our family tree. *My time would come, but it was not here yet.*

The Wilsons invited my whole family for Thanksgiving dinner. With their own family of four, they hosted my parents, my sister, her husband and son, my brother and his wife, and two students. Everyone was disappointed that I could not come along, but they made sure that I did not mind being left alone for a few hours. It was the first day that I was actually alone during visiting hours. It was a strange feeling, but I had a great deal for which to be thankful.

The day after Thanksgiving, a jovial, heavy-set man entered my room. From his thick foreign accent, I guessed that he was an Italian immigrant. He explained to my parents that he was the hospital barber. The doctors had sent him to cut my hair. They hoped that cutting my hair would decrease the irritation around my ear, which was infected.

I tried to peer into the case where he kept his scissors. When I did not see a bowl, I decided I would allow him to trim my hair—not that I really had a choice!

I was like a sheep being sheared of its fleece. With electric clippers, the barber shaved the sides of my head, and I felt naked. My head still rested on a pillow as he trimmed the sides of my head. Leaving the hair at the top and back of my head long, he managed to give me a Mohawk. Everyone laughed at my haircut, but no one dared show me a mirror.

Little did I know how avant-garde my hairstyle was. The barber had given me a punk haircut long before they became popular. It only added to my quirky presence.

Activities returned to the usual routine after Thanksgiving weekend. Life in the hospital was far from boring. Each morning I woke eager to see what advancements I might perform. Each day's improvement was small; perhaps I could move my arm two inches higher or my index finger slightly more than the day before, but to me the improvements were exciting.

Mornings were my favorite time of day, and they were too precious to waste. Like a baby, I was most alert and strong in the early morning hours. At no other time in my life had I looked forward to the start of a new day as much. The pain or coughing attacks were miniscule compared with the satisfaction of knowing I was progressing. I knew I could plateau at any time, but as I improved each day, I thought less and less about that possibility.

My body was no longer deteriorating; it was bouncing back. I could see the joy in other people's faces as they marveled at my recovery. Lisa was eager to arrive at the hospital each morning. She, too, wanted to revel in my improvements. Her face was bright with hope, pride, and love.

On her day off, Marilyn made a brightly colored chart for me so that I could tell when I was to have a specific therapy. The chart organized my day. The only problem with the chart was that it reminded me that I had respiratory therapy four times daily, seven days a week. Billy Feathers and most of the other respiratory therapists were entertaining, but I did not care for them pounding on my chest and then putting a suction tube down my throat to force me to cough, but I enjoyed their company, and they finished their chore quickly.

Some respiratory therapists, however, I dreaded. One female therapist loved to take her frustrations out on my chest and seemed to enjoy brutalizing me. She hit me harder and harder. After suctioning me, she would go for another round, sapping my energy to the point of exhaustion.

Lisa was in the room one day when the girl came. "You're hitting him too hard. Can't you see he's had enough?" she protested.

"I'm just doing my job," the therapist said. "It's good for him." Harder and harder she hit, and my body convulsed each time she suctioned me.

Lisa could no longer watch quietly. "Get out of here before you kill him," she shouted. "I'm going to make sure you never come in this room again!" She was as good as her word; the therapist was never assigned to me again.

Lisa and my mother did not often complain about the care I received, but they were effective when they did. One private-duty nurse fell asleep on night duty, manicured her nails and combed her hair constantly, and paid no attention to my needs. My mother was accustomed to the excellent care Fanny and the Four-East nurses had given me. When my mother spoke to the Personnel Office, the nurse was dismissed from my case.

My TV had a remote control. The remote was an old one, with a single button that advanced the channel selector. The channel selector only moved forward. Unfortunately, I did not have the finger control to manipulate the selector. I felt like Woody Allen in *Sleeper* trying to overpower a button, unable to master what seemed to be a very simple task.

Like something in a Japanese horror film, the selector button assumed massive proportions. I could not coordinate my finger to watch the desired channel. If I were lucky, I would release my finger a channel or two ahead of my desired channel, and I would earn another attempt before having to go all the way around the circuit again. Lisa enjoyed watching me struggle; she felt I watched too much TV. Only when she tired of watching each channel in two-second intervals would she help me.

Another favorite pastime was having Lisa read aloud. She read me my mail every day. She talked on the phone and corresponded by letter with many of my friends who realized that I was not able to communicate. Not all my friends wrote letters, but each supported me in his own way. I appreciated their efforts. As George Meredith wrote, "Friends are the leaves of the tree of life."

One of my friends, Andy, was off learning how to save the world in ten easy steps, as he put it, at the Fletcher School of International Law and Diplomacy. His letters always entertained me:

"I think the major problem with truth, especially political truth, is that it lacks drama….down the middle… so boring to write. No wonder the world is run by nuts, they are so much more entertaining than rational statesmen. And speaking of nuts, I spent a little time with Murphy."

He proceeded to tell me how he and Murphy, a college housemate and good friend, went on a rampage and somehow ended up driving Murphy's station wagon onto the lawn of a girls' dormitory at four in the morning.

Peter, my college roommate for four years, wrote to say he was organizing a safari to go after the "Great White Mosquito" that had bit me. Another friend, Jim, told me of the wine and women of California.

Lisa's other reading material was John le Carré's *Smiley's People*. Although the book was dramatic and exciting, I would often doze off with Lisa reading to me.

In physical therapy, I could lift my leg six inches from my bed. Anna, my therapist, would help me lift my limbs further. Anna could always feel the point where stretching the leg began to hurt, and she never went beyond that point. Still, by the end of the half-hour workout, I was exhausted.

In occupational therapy, Arlene was exercising my arms and fingers. She tried to get me to turn the pages of a magazine. She thought I might do better with *Playboy*, but decided to use *Sports Illustrated* instead.

My page turner was a stick with a soft rubber tip. The stick had an enlarged foam handle for easier management. I would balance the stick in the U-shaped area between my thumb and index finger. Resting it on my middle finger, I tried to apply pressure on the top of the stick with my index finger. Dragging the stick across the page would make it turn. In a fifteen-minute period, I would be lucky to turn one or two pages. Not the speed I needed to read an article, but I could no longer read. I knew how to read, but the time it took for my eyes to travel across a page made reading impossible. My eyes could not focus on a single word without my becoming dizzy.

The time in speech therapy with Jean was now spent learning to swallow solid food and preparing for the day when I would breathe without my tracheal tube. The first step in teaching me to swallow required Jean to spoon ice chips into my mouth. As the ice melted, I had to swallow. After a few days swallowing the chips, I advanced to Jell-O, not one of my favorite foods. The most positive thing about it was that each day it came in a different bright color. Jell-O was the first "solid" food I had eaten in two months. I looked forward to some pizza or a chili dog.

I could almost taste the Carson spare ribs or the Red Lobster "all you can eat" shrimp from the commercials on television. Even the McDonald's or Burger King hamburgers looked irresistible. Jean occasionally brought ice cream, but the ice cream melted too fast. From Jell-O, I finally advanced to yogurt—a big improvement—but I could still swallow only about one-fourth of an eight-ounce container each day.

In the weeks that my tracheal tube had been open, my body had become accustomed to getting oxygen directly into the trachea. I did not have to breathe through my nose and mouth, and had lost that ability. As my body gained strength, doctors were gradually becoming more confident in my ability to breathe on my own power. In order to force me to breathe on my own, Jean plugged a red stopper into the opening of the plastic tube in my throat. At first, I gasped for air as Jean plugged the opening for a few seconds. Gradually, she kept the stopper in place for progressively longer periods of time. I struggled for air at first, but slowly learned to relax and regulate my oxygen intake.

One day, the nurse who was training me left the stopper in place while she rushed from the room on an emergency call. She forgot all about it. For hours, I tried to remain calm and regulate my oxygen intake. If I started to gasp, I might never recover. I could not raise my arm to unplug it, nor shout for help. I concentrated on remaining calm. My frustration increased as other people entered and left my room, not realizing my concern. Finally, that evening another nurse noticed that the stopper was not scheduled to be in place, and I could breathe a deep sigh of relief. Perhaps the first nurse did me a favor, but her forgetfulness could have created a crisis.

Jean also brought me a communication board that had sixteen pictures, each with a descriptive word below the picture. A light flashed under each picture in sequence. Ideally, I would be able to stop the light below a specific picture, and the nurse would know what I wanted.

The problem with the communication board was similar to the one I had with the TV remote channel selector. I would light the picture for a bedpan when I actually wanted some yogurt. The communication board and I did not communicate.

Doctors visited often and asked, "How are you doing, Mark?" Of course, I could not respond. I suspected that some of them came in only to charge me for a three-minute visit; most of the doctors always came to the right side of my bed, and I saw their eyes floating as they talked with me. This observation tipped me to a second reason for their visits: the Playmate pin-up was hanging on the door to the left of my bed!

I had some excellent doctors, but interns did the bulk of the daily work that required contact with the patients, and it was with the interns that I developed the closest rapport.

The most unpleasant task assigned to the interns involved manipulation of the Darpov tube. A Darpov tube is a three-foot long tube that passes nourishment through a nostril into the stomach. The "nourishment" was a yellowish, milky fluid. The doctors blamed the formula for making me vomit seven or eight times daily. I often vomited so violently that I lost the Darpov tube. One day I lost it four times, upchucking it violently each time, so forcefully that once the tube tied itself into a knot.

Each time I lost the tube, my heart sank. An intern had to replace it. As the intern came into the room carrying a tube, I broke into a cold sweat. Placing his palm on my forehead, the intern said, "I don't like this any better than you do." He would then force the tube into my nostril, made more unpleasant because of my deviated septum. As the intern forced the tube, I could feel it work its way into my stomach. The tube might remain for two hours, or for two days; no one knew. Among other problems, the tube created a friction ulcer in my stomach, which made it necessary for the nurses to inject Maalox through the tube every two hours.

Around the middle of December, the doctors decided that I no longer required the room with a window running the length of the wall facing the nurses' station. I would move to a room across the hall.

"Look, it's snowing!" Lisa shouted. "It's the first snow of the season."

As I imagined the new falling snow and how cold and soft it would feel, I fell asleep.

## Chapter 7

# New Life

**M**y eyes flickered as I awoke. Nothing looked familiar. I was riding in a bus, but it was not a plush Greyhound. It was more like a converted school bus with its windows blown out. Some windows had been replaced with cardboard; others were left open to the elements. The bus was drafty and cold as we climbed a hill, but no rain came through the windows. Not yet, anyway.

Veiled women sat in the front rows, segregated from the men. The driver, his bandolier crisscrossing his chest, reminded me of Pancho Villa. I shook my head in disbelief. It seemed like a scene from the Old West. Beside me my friend, Dana, sat sleeping. An old man wearing a turban and sporting a long white beard sat across the aisle. His weathered hand held the steel barrel of an ancient flintlock rifle, the wooden stock resting on the floor.

Only stunted desert plants grew on the arid land, and I could see that the road ahead disappeared into ungracious mountains. I recognized the smell of gunpowder, and turned to see the old man loading his flintlock. He flashed a knowing smile, his teeth yellow but hard. The bus passed men sitting outside a solitary roadhouse, each carrying a flintlock similar to the old man's.

The old man saw that I was intrigued by the mystery of the razor-like peaks. He pointed to a cement outpost chiseled into the side of a mountain. "The Khyber has always been a battleground." His proficient English startled me.

I had read of the infamous Khyber Pass that lies between Pakistan and Afghanistan. Many powerful armies, from Alexander the Great to the British, had tried and failed to conquer the gorge that is said to be the gateway to India.

"The Great Khan did not even have much luck," the old man said.

"Tough terrain," I said.

"Tougher men," he replied. I was not about to disagree. "Pashtun bandits control the area, always have and always will. Pakistani authorities pay dollars to keep the Pass open. See the mountain up there to the right? That is the border to Afghanistan."

I wanted to continue with this scene from my past, but realized where I was, in a new room across the hallway. This room was much smaller than my old one. My bed almost touched the opposite wall, and the TV was now at the end of my bed, only eight feet away.

How will they fit everything and everyone into this room? I wondered. There's no room for Miss June. There's barely enough room for a chair for my mother. Well, I guess some things have to go. It's either Miss June or my mother. Not an easy choice! I loved my own jokes.

My bed was still at an angle, which prevented stomach acid from rising back into my throat. The nurses had made room for my IV, my feeding mechanism, and the machine used by the respiratory therapists that made my body spasm uncontrollably.

The snow had stopped, but clung to the edge of the window. The white snow seemed to give a fresh start to life, and I was eager to see what surprises the new day would bring.

I often woke in the dark not knowing where I was, or even in what time period I was traveling. Darkness was still a mystery, but it became my release. Lisa and the white walls were not there to anchor my thoughts. In my mind, I could leave the hospital and transform my body. I was no longer confined by movement. I could play basketball, golf, or pool, or travel to a foreign country to explore the vast unknown. No one could stop me. I was freer than I had ever been, and now I could appreciate that freedom.

Pain from being unable to shift my body brought me to the present. Not three feet away, Mrs. Torrez, my private duty nurse, sat knitting a sweater, unaware of my agony. *Doesn't she realize how painful this is?* I wondered. *If I could just get her attention, she could shift my body.*

"Oh, I see you're awake," she said. "How is my patient doing?"

Staring at her, I tried hard to send brain waves so that she could read my mind.

"Now, go back to sleep," she said, and I watched her knit the next row until she dozed into a world of her own. Mrs. Torrez never realized I was in pain. As she visualized it, her job was to sit patiently at my side while I slept blissfully until five in the morning, when she would sponge me, powder me and change the ribbon keeping my trach tube in place. Each night I hoped that she would not show, but for the two months she was my nurse, Mrs. Torrez never failed to miss one night, seven days a week.

Cliff replaced Fanny as my second shift private-duty nurse from 3:00 p.m. to 11:00 p.m. As my first male nurse, and the only male nurse on the floor, he was a welcome addition. Although we shared little in common, I felt comfortable with him. I could relax when a male saw me in my exposed, weakened state, while I felt vulnerable when a female saw me under similar circumstances.

Much to my mother's dismay, Cliff was not as cautious as the female nurses. One day while I watched a football game on TV, Cliff decided that I would benefit from an exercise trapeze attached to my bed. As he hoisted heavy metal poles above my head, my mother expected the worst. Cliff managed to rig the trapeze without a mishap, and it was a tool that I would never have discovered on my own. Each morning I would exercise my arms before breakfast. Eventually, the trapeze helped build the strength in my arms that finally enabled me to lift a spoon to my mouth and feed myself.

One of Cliff's major jobs was changing my bed sheets at least four times a day. He was strong enough to change my bed without any help; the same task usually required two or three female nurses to roll me over and change it.

Cliff had to do this unpleasant chore because the doctors were training me to control my urination. I would feel the urge to urinate, but often not in time to notify Cliff to place a urinal between my legs. I would wet my bed and feel guilty. Over the next several months, I learned to have my little blue urinal within my own reach. I could not always use it effectively, but it became an important symbol of freedom and independence.

Almost as unpleasant as having an intern insert a Darpov tube through my nostril into my stomach was having interns, male or female, extract urine for tests. Doctors could not wait until I had collected a sample in a plastic bag; instead, an intern would enter my room without notice, carrying a small white kit. After opening the kit, he cleaned the tip of my penis by swabbing the end of it with iodine. He then inserted a small plastic tube into the opening of my urethra. Once the tube arrived at its destination, pressure enabled the intern to tap a sample of urine.

Christmas was drawing near, and Lisa decided that my room should promote the Christmas spirit. Marilyn contributed a small artificial tree with blinking lights, and my mother hung a red and white Christmas stocking on the wall. Lisa draped red and green crepe paper from the ceiling, and placed a Santa Claus by the Christmas tree. She attached the hundreds of Christmas cards we received from well-wishers on the wall opposite my bed.

Later, Sam's mother brought an arrangement of evergreen branches and holly berries, and we still had the red poinsettia Lisa's mother had brought. But the many visitors really supplied the Christmas spirit, and the more people who came, the more Christmas spirit everyone felt. PJ, the female intern, told me that my room was by far the most festive place in the 500-bed hospital.

Anna announced one day that it was time to transfer to a wheelchair by standing up. I looked forward to standing for the first time in three months. I thought my body would be stiff as the rusted Tin Man in *The Wizard of Oz*, but I hoped that at least I would be able to support my own weight. I assumed I would be walking again in a matter of weeks, if not days. Anna tried to warn me that it might be longer, but I did not believe her.

Standing upright was another thrill in a rapid succession of many. Prior to this, the small movements I made had had a dramatic effect, but they were incomparable to the thrill of standing upright. Shaking my head "yes" and "no" had been an unparalleled development in communication. Controlling my index finger enabled me to press the buzzer to call the nurse and use the TV remote, but I was always dazed, always in a world different from the one I'd inhabited for twenty-five years. Even when I was consciously in the white, sterile room, I was always lying at a thirty-degree angle, and everything always had a glaze, a thin, surrealistic film. Now, lying in that bed, I was eager to see the world from a different perspective.

Anna sat me on the edge of my bed. I was already higher up than I had been in three months. She turned to lock my wheelchair in place.

Instead of being stiff, like the rusted Tin Man, I flopped like the

Scarecrow being released from his perch in the cornfield. My backbone could not support my weight, and I dropped back onto the bed like a felled tree. After righting me, Anna turned to find my shoes, but once again I flopped on the bed. My feet were too stiff for Anna to slide on shoes. She had to settle for bare feet, but she did manage to wrap a thick canvas belt around my waist. By grabbing the belt, she and a nurse could maneuver me into a waiting wheelchair.

On the count of three, they hoisted me to a standing position. For one brief moment, I looked out the window and down from the fourth floor onto the roofs of houses below. I saw smoke curling from chimneys and tall elm trees, their branches silhouetted against the gray sky and the blanket of snow. I looked down on the blinking Christmas tree and the dreaded suction machine. I towered above Anna and the nurse as though on stilts eight feet in the air.

"Say, you're a tall one," Anna said of my six-foot frame.

My knees buckled and my legs collapsed.

I could not understand how a girl so thin could be so strong. With the strength of a weightlifter, she guided my sagging body onto the wheelchair.

"There, how does that feel?" she asked.

I could not tell her how uncomfortable the chair was. My back, accustomed to the soft mattress, felt as if it were leaning against cement. With nothing to support my neck, my chin rested on my chest, and my head rolled onto my shoulder. My butt was sore after just two minutes. I hadn't weighed so little since I had returned from India as an emaciated nineteen-year-old. Lisa always had made fun of the fact that I did not have a rear end for girls to watch. My muscles had lost their flexibility, which made it impossible to fit my legs into the wheelchair. Instead of resting on foot pedals, I spread my feet directly onto the floor.

The first day, Anna kept me in the chair for only twenty minutes. By the second day, I was ready to try to sit for an hour. At the end of my half hour of physical therapy, Anna and a nurse transferred me into my wheelchair. To keep my feet warm, I wore socks. Anna reminded me that I needed a pair of shoes with rubber soles for the traction necessary for a safe transfer. Anna moved onto other patients, and the nurse attended to her other duties, but the nurse assured me that she would check up on me periodically.

I was not at all disappointed when they left me alone—I enjoyed the privacy. When the nurse first looked into my room, everything was fine, but by the time she returned ten minutes later, I had begun to tire. She did not notice that my head had started to droop forward.

Within two minutes after she left the room, my socks began to slide on the floor. As I grew more tired, my socks slid even more, and they dragged my tired body after them. I tried to brace my arms, but my feet powered my body. Another two minutes, and I was dangling between the chair and the floor. When the nurse returned, I was sprawled on the floor, laughing out of frustration and helplessness.

"Mark, what are you doing down there? Oh, you poor thing. Let's get you back in the chair." When she saw that I was unhurt, she could not hold back her own chuckle. With help from two other nurses, she pulled and pushed me back into the chair. "Now try to stay there this time, and I'll be back shortly." The nurse looked pleased. "Are you going to be all right?"

Unable to answer, I was already starting another slide by the time the three nurses left the room. Within minutes, my butt was nearly touching the floor. Finally, I could no longer prevent my fall and landed safely, if uncomfortably, on the floor.

A young hospital administrator entered my room, and I could see from her expression that she was surprised to see me on the floor. The young administrator had never met me before; she knew only that I had been very ill with some strange virus. Obviously new at her job, she tried to maintain her composure. The young woman was in my room to tell me that if I had any problems, to "let the administration know."

"Can't you see I have a problem now?" I wanted to shout. "Do you think I always sit on the floor?" No sound came from my lips. *Ahhh, get me out of this nuthouse if you want to help,* I thought.

The more frustrated I became, the more absurd the scene appeared, and the harder I laughed. Laughter made it impossible for me to signal for help. The more I laughed, the more insane I must have looked. The administrator stood in the doorway as the nurses whipped past her to my rescue. As nurses lifted my limp 140 pounds back to bed, the administrator left my room, still puzzled.

"Oh, what did you do to that poor girl?" a nurse pretended to scold. "She didn't know what to think."

I was venturing further and further from my bed, and the trips held unexpected adventures. Not unlike my travels to Europe and Asia, I was enjoying every minute of them.

Two days later, Jean thought I was ready to have speech therapy in the solarium on the sixth floor. Lisa wheeled me to the elevator, and I stared up from the wheelchair at the people we met. I was a strange sight for others, as Lisa had to cram my inflexible body to fit into the chair. My face remained distorted, and my disheveled punk haircut and wild-eyed stare added strangeness and mystery to my appearance. As people looked away uncomfortably, I had the opportunity to explore the wrinkles on their faces. I imagined all the suffering, the worry, the sleepless nights, and the age that deepened each wrinkle.

Before I knew it, we reached the solarium. As the solarium door was unlocked, a new world revealed itself to me. Sunlight streamed into the thirty-foot square room, and white snow increased the glare. *If only I had shades*, I chuckled to myself, *I would look real cool.* My eyes became accustomed to the bright sunshine, and as Lisa wheeled me forward, my arms seemed to float in the spacious new surroundings. Other hospital rooms where I had been were filled with equipment, but the solarium's only furnishings were couches and lounge chairs.

Lisa rolled me to a window, where I could look out over Lake Michigan. Even from that height, one could not see Michigan on the other side of the lake. I could see the campus of Northwestern University on its shores.

*Just think, there are probably people in the middle of final exams just about now*, I thought. *Thank God, I'm not one of them.*

I could see the buildings of downtown Evanston, and in the distance I could see the Chicago skyline, twelve miles away. Millions of people were living their lives within the scope of my view. How many of them had their own mountains to climb, obstacles to overcome? The mountain I was climbing was not much different from the mountains that other men and women were climbing. I did not envy the man struggling with unemployment, his recent divorce, or the loss of custody of his only son. I did not envy the woman confronting her depression and loneliness. Without a doubt I would choose my situation, with its challenges and excitement. My struggle was so visible, and I was the focus of so much goodwill. Love, concern and generosity flowed in my direction. Was that such a horrible position?

The major difference between my struggle and that of the man facing the recent divorce was that people were more eager to help me. In my case, if I grew frustrated and depressed, others were at my side to raise my spirits. The man reeling from more common misfortunes might not have support like mine.

As Lisa wheeled my chair to a shaded area, Jean gathered two chairs and was soon leading me in my daily speech calisthenics. "Scrunch up your face. Grimace," Jean directed. "Look lean and mean."

"Lean and mean! You know how to do that!" Lisa chimed in. I tried to imagine how Popeye would look with a hangover.

"That's it. Loosen up those muscles! One, two, three, one! One, two, three, two!" Jean counted. These were the kind of exercises I did not mind doing; not too strenuous. "OK, I want you to do at least ten of those. Now, stick your tongue out. Not at me! At Lisa. Stick it out to the right. To the left. Right, left. Right, left. Right, left," Lisa mimicked my actions as Jean directed us.

Jean put the red stopper into my trach hole. Without the stopper in place, it was impossible to regulate my air and speak. "Today, we are going to practice making sounds. I want you to repeat after me. Pa, pa, pa…ba, ba, ba."

It was the middle of December. I had not uttered a sound since entering the coma in September. The sounds did not come easily at first, and it was strange to listen to my own voice after such a long time.

"Mu, mu, mu…nu, nu, nu."

My voice did not sound even remotely familiar, and I strained to whisper each sound. At first, I thought the voice was coming from another body.

"See how you have to blow air out to produce the 'p' sound? Let's try it again. Pa, pa, pa … ba, ba, ba… That's better!"

For the next twenty-five minutes, we practiced more sounds. I grew bored with the la's and da's. I looked at Lisa out of the corner of my eye, and saw the sparkle in her blue eyes. She had come to my aid when I most needed her, and had sat faithfully by my bedside through the worst of times. Lisa had been an extension of me, serving as a tentacle into life beyond my hospital bed, a liaison between the world and me.

She later told me that she had thought, "I wish he would either die or get well. A girl my age is supposed to be going to wild college parties. Isn't that the way the script reads?"

I reached for her hand. At last, I could squeeze it, but I wanted to give something more to someone who had given me so much spirit.

"OK, say me, me, me, me…knee, knee, knee," Jean said.

"I, I, I …" I strained.

"What is he doing?" Jean asked.

"Repeat what Jean says," Lisa said.

"I, I, I …" I repeated.

"I think he's trying to say something."

"What is it, Mark?" Lisa leaned forward.

"I, I, I…love…you."

# Chapter 8

# A Gift

Those were the words Lisa had been longing to hear. Tears rolled down her cheeks, and she leaned over to hug me.

"Well, I guess I had better leave you two alone," Jean said as she quietly made her exit.

Lisa and I were both aware of the intensity of the moment. Those three words were the most meaningful I had ever spoken, and the most meaningful that Lisa had ever heard. The words released Lisa from the bondage of doubt, and showed my gratitude, trust, and respect. Her tears were a catharsis, and with them, tension left her face. At last, her lingering question was answered.

That afternoon, my father arrived from Maine. His presence was a big morale boost as well as a physical relief. I still could not lift my legs to shift them to a more comfortable position, but I could point to the area that was causing me pain. My father would vigorously massage my legs and start the blood circulating.

After he arrived, the nurses turned out the lights and lit a birthday cake they had gotten for my mother. The timing of the little party allowed the nurses from the first and second shifts to sing "Happy Birthday." They admired my mother's strength and courage, knowing that she was hundreds of miles from away from home. They had gotten to like and respect her during her two months with me on Four East. The nurses realized the sacrifice required to move from Maine to Chicago on a moment's notice, to rent a small apartment near the hospital, to find a job working mornings at the University, to buy a rusting Ford Pinto, and to stay with me daily for eight hours every day. In more than five months, she missed only one day, and that was the day before we returned home.

With the help of scrawls from her baby, my sister had made me a calendar for the month of December, each day marked with an individual drawing or saying. On December 18th, the calendar read, "Happy Birthday, Mom!" The calendar had given the nurses the idea to have a birthday party.

I was just beginning to reach the trach hole with my finger. By covering the hole, I was able to block the air flow and speak. News had spread rapidly that I had spoken that morning in speech therapy, and many of the nurses heard me speak later in the morning. Marilyn whispered to me to wish my mother a Happy Birthday, but I shook my head "no."

"Come on, wish her a Happy Birthday," Marilyn urged.

Again I shook my head "no," this time more emphatically than before.

Marilyn placed her own finger over my trach hole. "There, now say it to her."

Once again I shook my head.

"Why not say something?"

The party ended without me saying anything; I only shook my head "no" when one of the nurses urged me to say something. My mother was sincere when she told them that this had been the best birthday celebration ever. No one could understand why I did not wish my mother a happy birthday. The night passed, and I still had not uttered a word to her. My resolve and stubbornness were apparent.

The next morning, Lisa called Mom at her office. After Lisa finished telling her the results of some hospital tests earlier in the day, she said, "Someone would like to speak to you for a second."

"OK," my mother said, "put him on."

"H-h-happy B-b-birthday!" I squeaked as Lisa held the phone to my mouth.

Expecting a doctor on the other end of the line, my mother was shocked. Her birthday was that day, December 19th, and not the 18th, as the nurses had believed. My greeting was the first words she had heard from me in three months. The words would have been a gift to her the day before as well, but that was the way my mind was thinking, focusing on small details.

"What do you think of that?" Lisa asked gleefully.

"That is the most wonderful present I have ever received!" my mother said, trying to hold back tears.

The gift of those words was a form of repayment to her, and the timing was perfect. I enjoyed giving this gift more than any I have ever given her. Giving a part of myself that day was an enormous privilege.

On the 21st of December, I held up three fingers, but no one realized what I was trying to signal. My parents put the red stopper in my plastic trach hole, hoping it would enable me to explain.

"What are you trying to say?" my father asked.

"Three days," I strained.

"I know what he is trying to say," my mother said. "He's been in the hospital now for three months."

"A long time, isn't it?" my father asked.

I shook my head "no." That was not what I meant.

"What is it, then?"

"Insurance," I managed.

"No, don't worry about that," my father said.

"Three days left," I strained.

My family could not possibly afford my hospital bill. In my room across the hall, I had overheard Lisa and my mother reviewing the hospital costs. The room in ICU alone cost nearly $800 per day, even in 1980. Therapists, private-duty nurses, and doctors' fees were extra, not to mention each paper "chuck" or thermometer.

As a middle-class family, we had always managed to live comfortably. My brother and I had both gone to prep school on scholarships, and we all had received financial aid in college. None of us could have managed without sacrifice from our parents.

My parents valued education very highly, and they encouraged us to seek new learning experiences. Without their encouragement, it would have been impossible to travel to Barcelona, to go overland from Spain to Nepal, or to go to the Far East and Southeast Asia for a year and a half after college. My parents did not always agree with what I was trying to do, but they taught me independence and offered encouragement. At the expense of their own comfort, one of their top priorities was to educate me. I was determined that my family would not be in debt on my account.

"Three days left." Those words were etched upon my mind. I thought my insurance coverage lasted three months, and in three days it would be three months since I had entered the hospital. I lay in bed multiplying the costs as closely as I could estimate them.

I reasoned that I had three days to prepare myself before going home and regaining speech and movement on my own. If I never improved, I pictured myself like Christina in the painting "Christina's World" by Andrew Wyeth. Christina was the crippled friend and neighbor of Wyeth's in Cushing, Maine, whom he portrayed crawling alone in a field. If I had to, I could live as Christina lived, appreciating the magnificence of my surroundings. I spent many hours imaging how I would survive once I left the hospital.

I was wrong on several counts. My insurance coverage did not terminate in three months, and it was five days, not three days, until the three-month date. But if a situation ever arose that called for a sacrifice from me, I was ready to take whatever measures necessary.

Every second day, the IV nurse came to change the IV needle in my arm. The needle was inserted in a vein in my forearm, and a tube connected the needle to an IV bottle, which the nurses had to change every two hours. Each time a new IV needle was poked into my arm, it became more difficult for the technician to find a vein. Because my forearm had been punctured so often with everyone searching for blood, veins collapsed and became increasingly difficult to locate. In order to find a vein, the IV nurse often had to puncture my arm nine or ten times. An inexperienced nurse might give up after nine or ten pokes and leave to call a more experienced colleague.

I managed to communicate to Dr. Stand that the IV searches were quite painful. "If you can drink two quarts of fluid each day," he said, "I'll see what we can do about withdrawing the IV. We'll experiment with it for two days and see if you can do it."

Of course I can do it. Two quarts! I thought. Anything is better than having this IV stuck into my arm.

"Two quarts is a lot of fluid, you know," he warned. But I was ready to try anything.

By noon I had forced down a pint and already felt ready to explode.

"Here's another cup of apple juice for you," Lisa said, putting the cup on the table by my bed.

I was beginning to appreciate what Paul Newman must have felt like in *Cool Hand Luke* when he ate fifty hard-boiled eggs. As George Kennedy described it, he was "as ripe as a watermelon, ready to burst!" By nine o'clock that night, I finally had forced down the last drop of juice. For the first day, I had drunk my necessary two quarts.

I thought the second day would be easier, but the apple, orange, and cranberry juices started to lose their initial luster. I managed to consume two quarts each day for the next few days, and the IV stayed out of my arm permanently.

My body was taking a lot of abuse. I started to look upon it as a separate entity, not really as part of myself. I did not understand how my body could bounce back from being constantly probed and punctured. Technicians would tap blood samples for no apparent reason. Billy Feathers and the other respiratory therapists still came into my room and pounded on my chest to loosen up my lungs. I would still reel from coughing fits as the therapists poked a tube down my throat to suction me. I was worried about the apparent callous disregard both doctors and technicians had for the long-term effects of the procedures.

My deepest concern was x-rays. Nearly every day, an x-ray technician would enter my room wheeling a portable x-ray machine in front of him. I would be lifted, and the technician would put an inch-thick metal plate behind my back. As I rested against the hard, cold plate, the x-ray technician set up the portable machine and told me to "Say cheese," before snapping my picture. I used to worry when she would either leave the room or stand behind a lead shield. *If she needs a lead shield on the other side of the room*, I thought, *what do I need to protect me?*

Most of the x-rays were to check to see that the tubes forced through my nostril had made it to my stomach. On the worst day, my stomach rejected the tube four different times, and each time an intern had to replace the tube. The last time I lost it, my intern had to return to the hospital at 3:00 a.m. to do the unpleasant task, and with each replacement, an x-ray technician would have to take "pictures."

The next morning when Dr. Stand arrived, the intern told him that I had rejected the tube four times in the past twenty-four hours. But Dr. Stand had a pleasant surprise for me.

"That's not good, is it? What do you think about trying real food?" he asked, knowing how I would answer. "Do you think you can do it?"

"Yes," I answered enthusiastically. I had dreamed of pizza, Chinese food, and lobster. The dreams were as vivid as dreams I had when I'd raked blueberries as a boy. When I was twelve, closing my eyes each summer night after raking, all I could see were blueberries and more blueberries. This time, though, I welcomed the dreams.

As Dr. Stand pulled the tube hand-over-hand from my nostril, he ordered breakfast from the nurse. "Now, you have to consume at least twenty-five hundred calories per day. The nurses will measure all your calories," he told me. "That won't be easy, but I'm sure you can manage."

Breakfast arrived shortly, and Dr. Stand remained as the nurse fed me. The first thing I ate was a sweet roll. I almost bit off the nurse's finger.

"Slow down," Dr. Stand laughed. "Don't be so anxious." The sweet roll tasted like the best French pastry in Paris, not as if it had been mass-produced in a hospital kitchen. I wanted to slow down and savor each bite, but I was too eager for the next one. My cheeks puffed like a chipmunk's with a full mouth of acorns. The scrambled eggs might have been powdered, but I did not care. They were solid, delicious, and I ate them through my mouth; compared with the fluid draining into my nostril, they were exquisite. For lunch, Lisa and Marilyn brought me a piece of stuffed spinach pizza. Never before or since have I experienced such intense pleasure in eating. For the next few days I ate chili dogs, Chinese food, tacos, and whatever else Lisa brought into my room.

One day, one of the speech therapists came to observe me while I was eating. "How long have you been in the hospital?" she asked.

"Three," I strained.

"Three weeks. That's a long time," she said.

"Months," I corrected her.

The therapist looked surprised as she recorded the fact on her sheet.

As Marilyn fed me rice, I choked and started to cough, as I often did even when I was not eating. Because of the size, texture, and weight of rice, I had trouble eating it. I had more difficulty drinking water than milk for similar reasons. I could not always feel foods going down my throat, and I was still in the process of discovering which foods were best for me to eat.

"He should not be eating solid food. We'll put him on a pureed diet," the speech therapist said.

*Who is this bitch, anyway?* I wanted to say, shocked and disappointed. Part of my ability to progress as quickly as I did stemmed from my willingness to assume responsibility for some of my own actions. No doctors, nurses, or other therapists had ever mentioned changing my diet. I was annoyed that a young therapist could observe me for one meal and make a quick decision which would have a major impact on my life without consulting me or others.

The pureed diet was dismal and disgusting. No one could tell me that being depressed at mealtime was beneficial to my health. I debated whether the Darpov tube was preferable to the distasteful mush. The squash and mashed potatoes were not bad, but the pureed beets and spinach were unpleasant just to look at. And yet, the beets and spinach were not nearly as wretched as the pureed meat. To top it off, a restricted diet meant no salt or butter, but I had to force myself to eat to maintain my calorie count.

In the days before I could speak, Marilyn always joked that I would swear at her the first thing. I did not swear, but I was mad at Marilyn. My brother had sent a toy stuffed lobster to have everyone sign, and Lisa hung the lobster from the ceiling. Everyone who came into my room remarked on it. When the lobster first arrived in the mail, Marilyn called the lobster a crab. I was indignant, and after I began to speak, I set Marilyn straight.

"Not a crab, a lobster," I managed to tell her, with other nurses present.

"What? I don't know, crab, lobster, they're all the same to me," Marilyn laughed in front of her friends. "I'm from the Midwest, you know. I don't know about things like that!"

"Oh, no," I sighed.

That same morning Annette, one of the respiratory therapists, came into my room. I dreaded the respiratory therapists, even though I liked Annette as much as I liked any of them. Annette was quietly cleaning the suction machine when out of my mouth came, "I don't need you!"

Annette did not even know I could recognize her, and was shocked to hear a voice. Since I was the only other person in the room, it did not take her long to realize the raspy voice was mine.

"Well, you don't have to worry," she laughed. "I'm just taking this machine away."

I did not want to be blunt, but I wanted to make my point as clearly as possible. Welcome changes were happening rapidly.

Lisa was going home to Toronto for Christmas. One of the nicest Christmases either of us had spent had been just one year earlier in northern Thailand, where it had been just the two of us. She was scheduled to leave the day of the party, December 23rd. Sam was going to give her a ride to the airport, but for now we were alone and it was time to give Lisa her present.

My sister had a knitting business in Maine. Before I fell ill, I had remarked that I liked the color of one of her yarns, a hand-dyed wool from a local sheep farm. At Thanksgiving, Nancy recalled that color and offered to knit Lisa a sweater.

The gift made Lisa cry, but each of us sensed a new stage in our relationship. The irony lay in the fact that we were reluctant to have things change, even though we knew it was necessary. We were thankful that I had survived the last three months, but we realized that during that time we had been closer than ever before, or could ever hope to be again. An era in our relationship was drawing to a close.

## Chapter 9

# Where Is That Mosquito?

"**M**erry Christmas," my father said, standing at the foot of my bed. "They let you sleep late this morning, didn't they?"

"Yeah, I guess they did," I croaked, sounding as though I had a bad case of laryngitis.

"We heard on the radio that it's twelve below in New England," Mom said.

"I'm glad we're here," I said sincerely, not giving much thought to being in the hospital.

It was my idea of a near-perfect Christmas morning. Overcast gray skies and snow flurries offset the Christmas tree lights and added to the cozy warmth.

"What do you say we open the presents? I'm eager to see what you got me this year," my father joked.

It did not seem at all unnatural to be spending Christmas in the hospital. As a child, my Christmases were spent in snowy Maine, but when I was sixteen I celebrated Christmas in Barcelona, and when I was eighteen I listened to chants from the mosques of Istanbul. At twenty-three I was in Hong Kong, and at twenty-four I spent Christmas in Chiang Mai, Thailand. By now I was accustomed to these surroundings, my parents were present, the room was well-decorated, and there were lots of gifts under the tree. We were grateful to be in a warm room, and I shivered at the thought of the temperature in the Northeast.

The major difference from a usual Christmas was that I didn't have to get out of bed and go to the tree; the tree was already there. Also, I literally could not tear the wrapping paper without a struggle. After it took me fifteen minutes to open each of my first presents, my father grew impatient. "You look a little frustrated there, and being Christmas," he said, "I'll help you out."

That afternoon Dana came from St. Louis. We had known each other since shaking hands at four years old. We learned each other's strengths and weaknesses, rode third-class Indian trains together, trekked in the Himalayas, and dabbled in the Black Market in Kandahar. In Yugoslavia, we had shared a room in a private home with only one single bed for the two of us. We agreed that one of us would get the bed while the other slept on the hard tile floor, and made the decision, as we often did, by playing a game of cribbage, the winner getting first choice. Unfortunately, I had to sleep on the floor that night.

Dana's visits were not only an inspiration to me, but were also a support to my mother. In addition to Dana's visit, I received a multitude of Christmas phone calls, among them calls from Dana's twin brother, Mike, and other close friends from my hometown. My mother would hold the phone to my ear, and I would listen to everyone talk. I was too filled with emotion to talk back; I could only cry in response to their voices. Between the phone calls, Dana's visits, and the knowledge that my brother would soon be coming, I finally began to see my situation as others might visualize it. Since waking from the coma six weeks earlier, I had been progressing toward a day when I would be able to put the pieces together and understand the love and care others had shown me.

I had figured out before Christmas that I was in a hospital, but I had not completely understood how I had gotten into the hospital or why I remained there. The hospital had become my world, little different from other worlds to which I had adapted. On Christmas Day, I fully regained my consciousness. For the first time, I realized the extent of my illness and the sacrifices, energy, and genuine love everyone had shared with me. My heart seemed to swell throughout my whole body, filled with love like never before. I wanted to thank everyone, and express to them all the intense love and compassion I had for each of them.

When I say I am grateful to have had the opportunity to undergo this whole experience, I think of this time of love and compassion. Thrills like moving my finger for the first time, eating my first solid food, speaking my first words, standing or taking my first step were truly awesome and made the experience worthwhile, but this period when my heart swelled throughout my body made me question why I was the one lucky enough to travel this journey. Where is that mosquito, anyway? I want to thank him personally!

The experience left me drained and emotional. For the next several days, I would be having a normal conversation and begin to sob for no apparent reason. I would not cry out of sorrow; I cried for joy and gratitude, realizing others' sacrifices. At no other time since have I experienced such a wave of goodwill and love towards others.

The day after Christmas, doctors removed my trach tube and wrapped bandages around my neck to cover the hole that remained in my throat. Knowing that I no longer had the tube with the little red stopper gave me a psychological boost, and I hoped it would allow me to speak more clearly. I could talk more, but the bandages let air seep out, and made me sound like a radiator releasing steam. The hissing sound only added comedy to my strained voice.

That night my brother arrived from Toronto, later than we had expected. He had stopped in Detroit to buy me three bean burritos. The bean burritos were cold by the time he got to Evanston, of course, but he knew I loved them.

My parents left when hospital visiting hours were over, but John stayed until midnight, when the nurses finally had to ask him to leave. I drilled him with questions about the time I had spent in the hospital. Only then did I begin to put the pieces of my puzzle together. I asked about entering the hospital, and about what had happened. He told me about how my family, Lisa, and the Wilsons had responded to the crisis. He told me the doctors had been unable to treat my encephalitis, but focused on keeping me alive.

"They still don't know how far you'll recover, but now they are encouraged," he said.

"I still don't know anything about the period of time around October," I said.

"Don't worry about that," he said. "You didn't miss much anyway, that's a small price to pay. What you missed in quantity, you'll have to make up in quality."

"I'm ready for that," I said, but I still wondered about the lost time. I started to recall the life-like dreams I'd had. I remembered a rainy night in a migrant workers' camp filled with illegal Mexican aliens, trailers, tents, mud, and crying babies. I dreamed that I had to struggle along with the Mexicans for survival and to avoid immigration authorities, but my dreams had another dimension I did not fully understand. They were not fleeting images that slipped from my memory the night they occurred, as dreams often do; they were lasting memories.

I was in another dreamlike state after I woke from the coma. The world I saw from the hospital bed was like the world of the Mexican migrant workers—the major difference being that in the hospital, I was protected from the rain and the mud. When Mrs. Torrez tied my trach tube in the early morning, the nurse injected my arm, Billy Feathers beat on my chest, or a resident doctor said that he did not think I would make it, I lay wondering what world I would visit next. I always expected another world to appear; it was all part of the journey.

Dr. Stand was visiting relatives in Pennsylvania for the holidays, so I had to convince my intern to let me drink two beers a day, to help address my fluid intake on an experimental basis. My brother had brought a six-pack of Narragansett beer from the East to celebrate my return to better health. Narragansett is not a premium beer in New England, but was one of my favorites mainly because of the word puzzles on the inside of the bottle caps.

The day after John arrived, we sat watching a football game on TV. As was often the case, my big brother sat reading the newspaper. I sat in my bed sipping a flat Narragansett beer and eating my last burrito. It was so typical, I thought, watching football on TV, drinking beer, eating a bean burrito, with my brother totally ignoring me. This was something to celebrate: I had reached a point where my brother could take me for granted.

I had gained another dimension of awareness, and realized it was only a matter of time before I recovered more fully. But I had lost something, too: I no longer could float effortlessly from one world to the next. An immense barrier had returned between my world and the world of the Mexican migrant workers.

As we were watching football, David, a friend from Tufts, appeared in the doorway. He worked in a Boston bank, and was visiting his parents in the Chicago suburbs for the holidays. David entered my room with his head slightly bowed, carrying a bouquet of flowers. He had heard that I was deathly ill after waking from the coma, and he was surprised to find me laughing and hissing jokes in my Godfather-like voice, eating my burrito and drinking Narragansett. He did not know what to think when I started sobbing in the middle of a sentence, then switched to laughter a minute later. He soon understood that I was not crazy, but overwhelmed with emotion, and he joined in the contagious laughter.

The parade of visiting friends continued. Robert, whom I had met in Barcelona and lived with for a year at Exeter, came for a visit. He was a medical school student visiting his in-laws in Chicago. Robert always had a good story to tell, whether about the mountain tribesmen in Columbia or the jungles of New York City, and he always seemed to be rolling a cigarette. You could easily find him by following the trail of Bugler's tobacco. When he came to visit one day in Maine, my father asked him why he was wearing a heavy topcoat on a hot summer day. Robert explained that he had a hole in his floor board and he had to drive with the windows down. We all had a good laugh.

My daily schedule began to return to normal the next morning. Dr. Stand was returning from his holidays with relatives, and I was looking forward to greeting him when he arrived in my room. When he had left, I could barely talk; now he would be pleasantly surprised at my ability to maintain a conversation. I repeated to myself how I would welcome him back to Evanston and thank him for his important role in saving my life. By the time he arrived, I was so excited I couldn't speak clearly. Again, my room was filled with laughter.

Lisa came back from Toronto. In the four days she had been away, I had made dramatic progress, especially in my speech, and had also become much more motivated to exercise. When she'd left, I had not been interested in therapy of any type unless it related directly to everyday activities like raising my arm to feed myself, or standing to transfer into a chair. Now I began to set long-range goals. I placed more emphasis on strengthening my legs, making a direct connection between the strength of my legs and my ability to walk. I saw the therapeutic value of playing cribbage and putting my pegs in their proper holes. I could play only one street of cribbage at a time before I tired, but it was a beginning. I remembered the Chinese saying, "A thousand-mile journey begins with the first step." I was eager to take that first step.

Lisa and I decided to go downstairs to the snack bar on the ground floor of the hospital. I had heard how good their milkshakes were, but before I made the trip, Lisa wanted me to know what I was getting myself into.

"People aren't used to dealing with anyone in your condition," she warned. "They don't know what you've been through; they only see the finished product."

I was eager to start on our little journey. For the first time, I tried to wheel my own wheelchair. My left hand was stronger than my right, and I zigzagged my way down the hallway. Lisa would right my wavering course every ten feet until I reached the nurses' station, thirty feet from my door, where the nurses marveled at my recovery. We all had a good laugh about the path I had taken, knowing that I would soon improve.

In the snack bar, I felt strange and awkward. It was my first encounter with groups of people who had not been aware of my illness, and I felt people staring at me. My face was still distorted, and I had a unique haircut, but I soon recovered from my fear. When the waitress was impatient and rude to me, I felt more at ease.

On the 28th of December, a meeting was held to decide where I was going to go next. Would I stay on Four East, go to the Maine Medical Center in Portland, go to the Rehabilitation Institute in Chicago, or transfer to the Rehabilitation Unit in the Evanston Hospital, two floors away from my current home? Happy on Four East, I was apprehensive about the meeting and not eager to transfer anywhere. My room had become a temporary home, and I was afraid of any change.

Two doctors, Lisa, and my family were all scheduled to be at the meeting. The doctors were surprised when they entered my room and found a standing-room-only crowd. I had encouraged nurses, therapists, interns, and anyone else who might be remotely interested to attend the meeting.

Before making a final decision, I visited Rehab and decided it was worth a try. I began to look forward to the idea of a move at the first of the year. As my health improved, I was eager to see what the Rehab Unit had to offer. On January 2nd, I made the move to Two West, "Rehab."

## Chapter 10

# Doreen

She grabbed my hair and jerked my head back.

"Little bitch!" I wanted to scream.

Water from the shower was starting to splash into my trach hole. I gasped for oxygen and struggled to free myself, but Doreen had a fistful of my hair, and I still had very limited movement, and even less strength. I was too upset to talk, and had too little air to utter a sound. My dignity was stripped. I prayed for the water to stop, or for Doreen to slip, because she would never notice my struggle.

Doreen clutched my hair, rotated my head freely, and aimed my head so that the water from the shower splashed my face and entered my trach hole. Finally, she released my hair, and my head flopped forward. The cotton gauze bandage covering my trach hole was soaked, but it had saved my life.

Doreen had performed her early morning chore in a hurry, eager to finish her unpleasant task. As the gauze became soaked, more and more water entered my air pipe. While in a coma, I had often dreamed of drowning…

*I am floating down a river in the Middle East, the current carrying me towards India. Too tired to stay afloat, I begin to sink. I bob to the surface to see a junk sail by, and then submerge once more. Only my eyes rise above the surface, but I'm too exhausted to stay even that high. Suddenly, the river widens and I find myself stranded on a sand bar. I get up and stumble away.*

My dreams and the fear of drowning were still vivid. Doreen had been oblivious to my struggle. She did not look on me as an individual, or even as a human being. She thought of me as a patient, one of the many daily objects of her eight-hour labor.

Doreen's job that Monday morning was to transfer me onto a special plastic commode with wheels, and place me in line in the hallway where other bodies, clad only in sheets, waited to be hosed down by a nurse. In line with the other patients, I watched as my feet turned a dull purple caused by poor circulation and the cold. As the line moved, nurses wheeled other purple, shivering bodies back to their rooms. Some would protest, while others sat in silence, their chalky bodies slumped forward as if huddling from the cold. Nearly all the others were elderly stroke patients who were even colder than I.

*Take me back to Four East,* I thought. *Aw, please take me back to Four East.*

I had moved to Rehab on Sunday, January 2, and realized that I had reached a new plateau. On Four East, I had been comfortable with the routine, the surroundings, and the nurses. My single room was always active, and it had become a favorite place for the nurses to gather. Many of the nurses on Four East were in their early twenties, and I had a great deal in common with them. Nurses in Rehab were older and less vivacious. Many of them were kind, but much more businesslike than my previous nurses.

The nursing staff on Rehab had one special plus over Four East: three male nurses in their mid-twenties. The male nurses, however, were low in the power structure's pecking order.

Hot, stuffy air greeted me when I entered my new room that Sunday. The room had two empty beds, and I chose the one near the window. To my disappointment, the window did not open.

"Can you turn down this oppressive heat?" I asked.

"Sorry, we've been trying to get them to regulate the heat, but they don't do anything about it," the nurse said. "I think the thermostat must be broken. Sometimes it's real hot and sometimes real cold."

"It's like a greenhouse in here," I said.

"Well, I'll see what we can do about it," the male nurse seemed sympathetic.

"Do you think it might be possible to get an exercise trapeze over my bed?" I asked.

"Sure, I think we can have that up this afternoon," he said.

I was beginning to feel more comfortable about my change to Rehab, but this was only one nurse. "I like to do arm exercises every morning before breakfast."

Meanwhile, Lisa was facing her own struggle. Should she return to McGill University in Montreal?

"If you don't go back now," I argued, "you may never go back, and I kind of worry about that."

"Why should I go back?" Lisa fired back. "I hated school in Toronto, and I don't know why McGill will be any better."

"You're right," I said. "It may not be any better, but you'll never know that unless you give it a try."

"I'll take my chances. I don't want to leave you here alone," she said.

"You know I'll be all right," I said. "You may not regret it now, but if you don't return to school, are you going to resent me for that in ten years?"

"You don't want me to stay here, do you?" she cried.

"Of course I do. You can't imagine how much I'll miss you. Just think how boring it will be around here when you're gone," I said.

"That's for sure!" She was beginning to lighten up.

"I just don't want you to be thirty and blame me for your not going to college. One day when you're a little older, you'll wake up one morning and leave me in the dust, and I'll be stuck with two crying kids!"

I could sense her agreement. "What if I like those other guys better?" she asked.

"As if," I said. "Listen, the more you see of other guys, the more you're going to appreciate me." Here I was sitting in a wheelchair, wearing ugly sweatpants that were six inches too short, with a whacked-out haircut and a droopy face, my blue security urinal at my side, a bandage around my neck, and hissing air when I spoke.

"Jesus, you're cocky, aren't you?" She shook her head.

I did not want Lisa to leave, but I knew she had to. Down deep she knew it, too, but she was apprehensive about leaving a secure world where she was never alone to go to an unknown one where she would be. We both knew we were on treacherous ground.

Lisa was my closest connection with the outside world. She was my mouthpiece when I could not speak, and was my best incentive for getting well. I hoped I was prepared to care for myself; if not, I would have to learn to be. I had to retain my independence, and Lisa deserved her own life.

If I had asked Lisa to stay, she would have, but I encouraged her to go. She had seen many things that most people never experience in their lifetime, but there were other experiences she had missed. She deserved to go to new places, meet new people, and go out with new men. Looking into each other's eyes, we made an unspoken pact. I felt the weight of another life on my shoulders, but it was not a cumbersome burden. It was a life that I loved very much, and I could not take the responsibility for entrapping her in a life that was for the moment centered within four hospital walls.

Tears poured uncontrollably from my eyes as Lisa left on the morning of January 5th, three days after my arrival in Rehab. My crying only made the departure more difficult for her. We were not breaking up, but we both realized that a new stage in our relationship loomed. I was proud of her for staying by my side during such a difficult and trying time. Now that I could communicate, I hoped her physical presence would not be as crucial as it had been.

Lisa left in the morning. By noontime, I needed her to protect me again. Doreen burst into my room and started wheeling me into the hallway in my chair.

"Where are you taking me?" Silence. "Doreen, where are you taking me?" I wanted an answer, and her silence made me apprehensive.

"You're on the list to eat lunch down in the lounge with the others," she finally said. "All people on the list must eat down there."

"I don't want to eat down there," I managed to say. "They all smoke." What's more, I ate at my own slow pace so that I would not choke. Other people always lit cigarettes well before I had finished, which irritated my throat with my open trach.

"You're on the lunch list, and so you have to eat in the lounge with the others," she said again. "This is Rehab."

As the wheelchair rolled forward, I protested, but she ignored me. I grew more angry and excited, and it became impossible for me to speak for lack of oxygen. I finally managed to blurt, "I don't want to go!"

The wheels of my chair kept turning. Doreen pushed me forward as if I had no say in my own destiny. My protests faded when I realized that my attempts to communicate with her were futile. *If only Lisa were still here, she would never have let this happen*, I assured myself, but it was time for me to handle my own problems.

That afternoon I explained to my occupational therapist, Arlene, that it was important for me to eat lunch without the distractions of others, and that smoke bothered me. She listened to my complaints with sympathetic ears. That alone was important, because it alleviated my fear that I was losing control of my independence and my destiny. Arlene saw to it that I was removed from the lunch list. She told me I could eat in my room.

I was still angry about Doreen wheeling me to lunch. My body was not accustomed to sitting in a wheelchair for hours, and it was aching. I was grateful for the strap around my waist, which prevented me from sliding out of the chair and onto the floor.

It was three o'clock in the afternoon, and my next big event was dinner at five. I wanted to lie down and take a nap before dinner. After rising at six thirty that morning, experiencing the emotional trauma of Lisa returning to Montreal, and a full day of therapy, I deserved it.

I pressed the buzzer to call the nurse to help me back to my bed. My tired body was beginning to slump forward with fatigue. Lisa could have transferred me to the bed, but Lisa was gone.

"What do you want?" an impersonal voice asked over the intercom.

"Would someone please help be back into bed?"

I waited for more than twenty minutes for the voice to respond. They must have forgotten about me. I pressed the buzzer again.

"Yes, can I help you?" Once again the voice spoke over the intercom.

"Will someone come help me to bed?" I was growing desperate.

"I'm sorry, you can't go back to bed," the voice on the loudspeaker said.

"What do you mean I can't go back to bed?" I was incredulous.

Another voice came over the speaker. "Mark, it's too early for you to go back to bed. You have to wait until after dinner."

"But I can barely sit in this chair." My voice rose with anger. "I'm so tired."

Cathy, my primary care nurse, came to my room. "Mark, we have to teach you to stay up," she said sternly, but compassionately. "You're in Rehab now, not on Four East."

My voice flared with outrage. My indignation rose. "You're trying to break my spirit. Don't call that rehabilitating me!" My voice strained, and I concentrated on regulating my air. When I talked I sounded like Marlon Brando in *The Godfather*, interrupted by an occasional hiss from the cotton gauze bandage wrapped around my neck. "Who do you think you are, telling me I can't go back to bed and take a nap before dinner? This is my life you're playing with!"

"My hands are tied. What can I say?" She shrugged.

The argument continued for fifteen minutes. Cathy was softening, but I wanted to clear my chest, and finally had someone in Rehab who would listen.

"OK, OK, we'll compromise. I agree to transfer you back to bed if you agree to get up later. Is that a deal?" Cathy offered.

"Of course, I'll get up later." I was still flushed with battle, and victory felt good. "Do you think I want to go to bed at three in the afternoon?"

"You'd be surprised, I think, how many of the other patients don't want to get up once they return to bed," she said.

After my argument with Cathy, I had only minor problems with the other nurses on Rehab. Word must have spread, because after that incident, the nurses always thought twice before they suggested I do something. They realized I cared more than anyone else whether or not I got well, and they learned to assist my progress, not impede it. The argument was also a milestone in my personal growth. I had voiced my own opinion and stood up for my rights, something I had not done since I'd entered my coma three months earlier.

## Chapter 11

# Decisions, Decisions

It was the sound of bells I had been fearing. The faint jingling of the bells announced the arrival of a donkey train approaching us on the trail.

I was trekking in Nepal, traveling in my past. The trail was chiseled into the side of a cliff one hundred feet above the roaring Khali Kandaki River, crashing into boulders as it raced down the valley. The trail had narrowed to about four feet wide and five feet high. The height of the trail was closing in on me, being six feet tall, and I saw the red feathery headgear of the lead donkey only a hundred yards in the distance. It was too late to turn around and try to outrun the train; with packs, we were no match for the agile donkeys that were carrying supplies to Mustang and Tibet in exchange for salt.

We huddled together against the inner wall until the fifty donkeys and their three handlers had passed. We decided to press on, not sure what lay ahead. As we trekked forward, the trail narrowed considerably, to only two and a half feet across. The Khali Kandaki boiled like a tempest almost ninety feet below us. Panicking, we talked about turning around, but our metal-framed packs made that tricky and dangerous.

Dana, Nancy, and I turned a corner. Only eight feet in front of us, the trail led out over the cliff for a foot, but it was a very long foot. The gravel beneath us was loose and crumbly, and the roar of the river was deafening. The trail narrowed to two feet, and there was a space of a foot where the crumbly gravel had eroded. A short distance ahead, the trail widened. I wondered how the donkeys with their heavy loads had passed this point.

I fought the urge to look down and forged ahead until I reached a point where I could lend Dana a hand. Within an hour we reached our destination, giddy from excitement.

"OK, Mark, time to wake up," the nurse said.

Before I could open my eyes to see who was speaking to me, a thermometer was stuck in my mouth, and the Velcro strip of a blood pressure gauge was fitted snugly around my bicep.

"What time is it, anyway?" I asked, rubbing my eyes.

"It's six o'clock. Time to get up."

By six thirty the race was underway. The nurses placed their patients in the cattle line, waiting for the one available shower. I preferred to be first, avoiding a long wait in the frigid hallway. Also, being first let me be one of the first people the occupational therapists taught to dress themselves each day.

Dressing myself took practice. I would lie on the bed and roll around until I managed to hoist my pants up over my hips. My muscles were too tight to reach my feet, and the therapists had to put on my socks and shoes. Once the therapists tied my shoes, I was ready for breakfast at seven thirty.

After breakfast, my first exercise of the day was hallway laps in my wheelchair. I had difficulty wheeling my chair in a straight line at first, and usually found myself at a dead end facing one of the walls until a nurse corrected my course. Once I learned to coordinate my feet by walking them in front of the wheelchair, I was able to use my arms and legs to gain speed and control.

By 9:00 a.m. I was ready for speech therapy, but regaining my speech was low on my priority list. Learning to regulate my air to form the correct sounds did not seem as important to me as learning to walk. Speech will have its time, I thought, but that time is not now. Speech was never mentioned as a deterrent whenever I asked my doctor when I could leave the hospital.

At 9:45, a transport aid would wheel me to physical therapy, where I worked with Anna. Physical therapy did affect when I would be able to leave the hospital, and it was physical therapy where I expended the most effort. The doctors said I could go home when I could rise from the wheelchair and make it to the bathroom without aid.

Anna was very instrumental in improving my physical health, but she was more important in improving my mental health. Anna listened to me, and in the hospital, it was rare to have someone listen. As she stretched my muscles, we discussed the problems I was facing. She empathized with me about the trouble I was having with the Rehab nurses, and intervened when possible.

I was back in Rehab by 11:15. I could not read, and I was too tired to exercise, but I did not want to return to bed, so I would go to the lounge and watch TV. The lounge was usually empty in the morning, and it was my favorite time of the day to spend there.

Lunchtime was usually uneventful, but one day Sam and the Dean came to visit. They often stopped by during their busy school day, but it was not usually at lunchtime.

"Hey, I see we're just in time!" the Dean joked from behind the curtain.

"You mean to check out some of the nurses?" I rasped.

"No, I mean for lunch," he said. "What are we having?"

As often happened, I liked my own joke and started laughing, but could not control my reaction. Within a minute, my lunch gushed out of my mouth and over the front of my shirt.

"We did want lunch, but not that badly," the Dean said.

"I didn't have anything left to share!"

After lunch, I visited Arlene in occupational therapy, who worked mostly with my arm muscles and fine motor skills. I spent countless hours putting pegs in their holes, stretching my arms, or relearning to write and catch a ball. At least, I tried to play catch, but the ball would usually career off my chest as I clapped my empty hands.

Like Anna, Arlene was important to my mental health. Her humorous conversations were lively and stimulating, but more importantly, she listened seriously to what I said. Other patients received only half an hour each of PT and OT, but I was progressing rapidly, and they let me stay longer. Doctors and therapists feared that my progress might stop with inactivity. Anna allowed me to have an hour of PT in the morning, and Arlene was happy to have me spend all afternoon in OT if I wanted.

After dinner, I wheeled laps in the hallway. The lucky patients who could practice walking practiced with a nurse, and I was eager to be one of those.

My original goal was to walk by my birthday, January 10th. The doctor had said, "If you keep that up, you'll be walking in a month."

"A month?" I was incredulous.

"Yes, you're coming right along," he said.

"I'll be walking in a week," I assured him.

"We'll see," he answered as though he knew something I did not.

I expected my muscles to rebuild strength rapidly, but it was a slow process. I began to revise my expectations. With Anna's help, I settled on a more realistic goal of walking the length of the parallel bars and back to my wheelchair by my birthday, January 10th.

As my birthday approached, I was still far from my goal. The preceding Saturday, two days before my birthday, I still had not been able to walk back to my wheelchair. On Monday, Dr. Stand came to physical therapy to watch, aware of my goal. With an extra day's rest, and the added incentive of his attendance, I made it back to my wheelchair easily. I beamed with pride at my short but gigantic accomplishment.

Although my progress seemed slow, I was eager to push ahead, and the more physical improvements I made, the more my desire grew for other overall improvements. It was like hiking up a mountain, and around each bend was a spectacular view. As in Nepal when I climbed higher, the view became ever more expansive, and I was drawn to greater heights. My "view" in the hospital was a sense of accomplishment, and each accomplishment pushed me forward to another.

On my birthday, my mother came by early after lunch to wheel me to OT. Marilyn, Anna, Arlene, and the other OTs were eating their lunch in the OT kitchen.

"OK, here's the birthday boy," Arlene said. "We have a little surprise for you." She opened the door to the oven, and pulled out a birthday cake with one candle on it.

"We could only find one candle," Marilyn explained.

"Make a wish and blow it out," Anna said.

I blew, but the flame only flickered. I gathered all the wind I could muster and tried to coordinate my breath. Again, the flame only flickered.

"Aw, it's a trick candle," I said.

"No, it isn't," Arlene said.

"It really isn't, Mark," Marilyn said. "Here, we'll hold it closer. Then maybe you can get it."

I blew again with all my strength. Nothing. I swelled my chest and blew again, but by now I was exhausted. The candle burned low before the therapists all helped.

My body was still stiff, and my muscles were tight and inflexible. The only walkers available were too short, so I had to wait for a higher, personally fitted model. When it finally arrived, I was like a racehorse in the starting gate, waiting to be released and let free to run. With the assistance of the walker, I walked from the room where Anna gave me PT into the main OT room, a distance of approximately twenty feet. I loved the feeling of being freed from the wheelchair and its confines, but the walker felt light and shaky. Anna held a strap around my waist, and someone followed behind me, wheeling a chair in case my legs collapsed.

The next Sunday, Dr. Stand allowed me to go to the Wilsons' for dinner. It was the first time I had been outside since the previous September, a period of more than three months. I brought my trusty blue urinal and an extra pair of pants in case I did not react quickly enough. When the Dean arrived to meet my mother and me, I had been ready for two hours, excited about my first venture into the fresh air. The Dean transferred me into the passenger seat, and my mother sat in the back.

"We won't be eating for awhile, so why don't I give you a tour of Northwestern, and then we'll go in to Chicago," he said. I had only been in the Chicago area for a few days before I entered the hospital, and was eager to see more of it.

We drove first to Northwestern, and he began to point out the different parts of the campus. "Over here is the Allen Center, and over there is the Library." My head swiveled to see the buildings he was pointing out, but my eyes could not adjust quickly to even the slightest movement. I could not read a newspaper paragraph without my feeling sick. I tried to look straight ahead to control the motion discomfort in my stomach. Things were whirling around outside.

"I'll drive you down to Chicago if you want to see that," the Dean said.

"Sure, we'd love to go," my mother answered, not realizing my anguish. It was a pleasant change for her.

We had not gone far before it was too late to ask the Dean to pull his car over to the side of the road, because I could no longer talk. I vomited all over his front seat.

"I expected this might happen," the Dean said, trying not to appear upset as he cleaned the front seat of the car. "Actually, I'm not surprised at all."

I was surprised, however, and very embarrassed. It had been several years since I had vomited as a result of motion sickness, and this was the Dean of Students of my school. Luckily, I'd brought that extra pair of pants.

I felt much better as we continued down Lakeshore Drive into Chicago. It was not long before I felt uncomfortable again, but we reached the Dean's home without incident.

On the first night Anna granted me permission to practice walking with a walker in Rehab, I almost made it to the door of my room, a distance of six to eight feet. I was tired after a long day of rehabilitation, and my muscles had very little stamina. The nurse guided me by the belt strapped around my waist, and my mother followed behind, wheeling my chair. The second night I walked with the aid of my walker to the door, and the next night I made it into the hallway, about five tile lengths from my room. I was like a young boy learning to walk on stilts, but the stilts were my legs. I looked forward to walking each night, but I had only one chance a night, and I had to make the most of it.

By the fourth night, I wanted to walk to the corner by the nurses' station, about twenty feet from the door to my room. When I reached the door, I began to tire. I was afraid that it would not be my night to reach the corner. I expended a great deal of energy just walking the first five tiles. My legs started to shake after ten tiles. I had already surpassed the previous night. I wanted to sit down, but something would not let me rest.

Several nurses were watching from around the nurses' station. "Come on, Mark," they urged. Other patients and their families gathered to watch. Was it sweat or tears that were causing my eyes to water? The shaking in my legs grew worse as I weakened. It was as if everyone willed me the next ten feet. With all their help, I made it to the corner. It was the longest walk of my life.

# Chapter 12

# The Final Days

As soon as I reached the corner, I motioned to my mother for the chair. Without waiting another second, I plopped into the seat. The events of the night overwhelmed me and added to my weakened state. I bawled like a baby. Understanding my embarrassment and my need to escape the scene, my mother quickly wheeled me back to my room.

My frustrations with the Rehab nurses continued. I could not understand how every other day they would lose a piece of my clothing in the wash. It would not have been quite as unusual if it were not for the fact that for much of my stay I was the only young man on the unit, and nearly all of my clothes had tags with my name clearly printed on them. How could my clothes be confused with those of an 80-year-old lady? My annoyance grew disproportionately because I had little else to concern me in Rehab.

My greatest frustration was more serious. Sitting in a wheelchair, I needed help to get to the toilet. All my muscles were extremely weak, including those that controlled my bodily functions. At times, I could not control myself, and had an accident before I could put my urinal in place. I would sit in my room and press the buzzer to call a nurse, too embarrassed to venture into the hallway. Sometimes I would wait only five minutes, but more often the wait would be thirty to forty-five minutes—if, indeed, a nurse came at all. I would sit endlessly in wet pants, feeling ashamed that as a 26-year-old man I had to wait for some nurse to come change my pants while the toilet was only ten feet away.

Sam and his roommate, Jeff, invited me for Sunday dinner in early February. I had not been out since going to Dean Wilson's, but my reputation as a prolific vomiter had spread, and we were all very conscious of the threat of my getting sick in Jeff's Buick. Sam and Jeff lived in a second-floor apartment, but it presented no problem as they simply carried me up the stairs as though I were a piece of precious furniture. They were afraid of dropping me, but I had confidence in them and laughed at their anxiety. Having to rely on other people so often, my radar had become acute, and I knew that I could trust Sam and Jeff.

A friend of theirs stopped by and ate some birthday cake with us. Sam had turned 26 two days earlier. It was awkward for me to be around men my own age outside the hospital. My life had changed, and I was slow to adjust to the new environment, but Sam and his friends were patient and understanding. We went to see the movie "Fort Apache, The Bronx." With its scenes of violence and sex in the New York ghettos, the movie was an abrupt change from the pristine hospital environment.

Dr. Stand invited my parents and me for dinner one evening. I had never met his wife or his baby daughter, who had been born while I was comatose. I had seen pictures of her, watching her grow while knowing that her life had started while I lay unconscious. Babies held a special fascination after my coma, because I was learning to move in much the same way as they were.

Leaving Dr. Stand's home, we had a chance meeting with one of his neighbors. "We prayed for you in our group every week," he told me. I was awed by his sincerity; how lucky I was to be the focus of so much goodwill from so many people I had never met. The loving spirit, caring, and honesty were inspiring. Never before had I even met Dr. Stand's neighbor, yet he had taken the time and energy to pray with others for me.

I received visits and letters from various church groups, but Christians were not the only ones who offered spiritual assistance and brought me into their homes. Zen Buddhists chanted for me, Jewish friends traveled great distances to visit me, and both black and white nurses put their hearts and souls into caring for me. People back home provided support to my mother with their prayers, notes, and gifts of money. The list went on and on. It was an enormous privilege to experience such an outpouring of goodwill. It did not matter what people's beliefs or backgrounds were: so many had given so much. It was overwhelming. A part of each one had become part of me. My struggle was not mine alone. I was driven by a desire to fulfill the hopes of others. I did not want to disappoint anyone. The excitement I saw in others' faces spurred me on to new heights.

Lisa and I talked on the phone often. She was having problems adjusting to college life. Lisa had had a devastating experience, and was emotionally worn out. When she thought of me back at the Evanston Hospital, it was especially difficult for her to concentrate on her studies.

Lisa was my main incentive for getting well, and she knew that. Without constant attention, I had a tendency to sit back and procrastinate. While others would congratulate me on my progress, Lisa was never satisfied, and knew when I was not truly satisfied, either. I would try to impress her with my advancements, but she would ask, "Have you walked to the bathroom yet?" In her own way, she was unrelenting and impatient, and I felt that she had a reason to be.

Both of us were growing emotionally drained. Neither of us understood why I was not progressing faster. I needed a new, more stimulating environment.

By the end of February I could easily walk with the aid of my walker to the lounge and back to my room. Rising from the wheelchair was getting easier, and I could even read a short article in the newspaper without growing dizzy. I was much more stable on the walker, and often bolted without anyone guiding me by the strap around my waist. I was no longer afraid of falling while walking with my walker.

One evening I went to the Wilsons' armed only with my walker, and, of course, my trusty blue urinal. Even the urinal was outliving its usefulness. There were few daily landmarks. I continued to progress, but it was not as exciting as it had been. It was time for a change and new challenges. It was time to go home.

## Chapter 13

# Blowing in the Wind

The countdown began when the plane took off from Burlington, Vermont. The flight from Chicago stopped in Vermont on its way to Portland, Maine, and once the plane left Burlington, the flight to Portland would last only twenty minutes. My palms began to sweat with excitement and anticipation as we neared Portland. Lisa was waiting at the Jetport. A wave of relief rushed over me as the wheels finally touched the runway.

The more often I flew, the less I liked it. It might have been the flight into South Korea that made me dislike flying. As we flew into Seoul, thunderstorms had rocked and rattled the airplane in a thick bed of flashing clouds. The clouds had seemed to have a will of their own as they tossed the airplane from side to side like the silk of a milkweed pod. I had been on rough flights before, but when the plane landed, it belly-flopped onto the runway, jostling the passengers in their seats. Had it been my imagination, or did we skid to a halt? Were those Korean rescue vehicles waiting for our arrival? Then, immigration officials had frisked Lisa and me as though we were dangerous criminals. I imagined the Korean secret police watching our every move from behind their sunglasses. Lisa had instinctively reached for my hand as agents scrutinized our belongings.

Immigration released us after an hour, but we were the last passengers of the day in the terminal, and Seoul had a 10:00 p.m. curfew. We waved down the last taxi, and the driver agreed to take us the seven miles into the city. We drove past city roadblocks that would form in five minutes, racing down deserted city streets to our hotel. We tipped the driver generously and hurried through its doors, Lisa still recovering from her fright. That was one of the many experiences that bound us together. Now she was waiting for me at the Portland Jetport, and I had trouble containing my emotions.

There was no sleeve to load or unload passengers from the plane, and when I disembarked that cold, foggy March night, I immediately noted the smell of salt air. I had missed it in Chicago.

A porter met me at the plane with a wheelchair. Anticipation grew as he wheeled me into the airport gate. Lisa came running out to meet me; I was too excited to speak. Crying was my only emotional outlet, so the tears flowed freely once again.

After more than five months, I felt relief at being back in Maine. No longer confined within the hospital's white walls, I felt comfortable in a familiar environment. The change gave me an incentive to improve.

My sister brought her nine-month-old son, Bubs, home the next weekend. Nancy helped clarify my perspective. As a Zen Buddhist, she had some practice trying to understand transcendental experiences similar to my own. She helped me realize that I was fortunate to have had such a unique experience, and one from which I could learn so much. It would take time to gain a clear perspective, she told me, but she was confident that I would see it as a great experience. "At least an unforgettable one," she joked.

I had already gained a new perspective on life, a side of life not often seen, but I could not put my feelings into words. Most people saw it as so devastating that they were reluctant to hear anything positive about it.

Being the focus of so much positive energy had a powerful effect. My senses were heightened, humor more intense. Even some of Dean Wilson's jokes seemed funny! My overwhelming feeling of goodwill toward others would have a lasting effect, and I would never forget the pleasure of tasting my first morsel of solid food or speaking my first words.

Sometimes I think the experience was hardest on my family and Lisa. They were the ones who'd had to watch me lying in a comatose state for weeks and later being locked-in, not knowing what the result would be. I only saw myself improving. I never doubted the fact I would recover. Everyone else had gone through a period of great stress and doubt, but I never had to face that doubt as they did, or to ask myself, "What kind of shape will I be in if I do survive?" In some ways, mine was the easiest role of all.

Most of all, I wanted to satisfy Lisa and my family. I sensed their will-power spurring me on when I had little of my own. Their hopes and pride were riding with me. If they lost me as a son, a brother or a boyfriend, they would lose a part of themselves. I was not going to let that happen. I felt everyone believed that if they tried hard enough, I would survive and recover. I had little choice in the matter. I had to do my part.

Once therapy started, my improvement was rapid. By the end of March, I could launch myself from a chair if it had armrests, and could walk up and down the three front steps of our home with a cane.

Then Lisa dropped a bomb on me. One I had been expecting, but it was still a tremendous jolt when it hit. She was interested in another man in Montreal. Lisa did not realize how natural it was for a college freshman to lead a life of her own, away from the hospital and therapy, especially as Gardiner was a seven-hour drive from Montreal. Lisa was confused about her feelings, and hoped that I could shed some light on them.

I did feel abandoned at first, and wanted to add to her feelings of guilt. Lisa was the one bright spot in an otherwise boring schedule. I looked forward to talking with her on the phone, to checking the mail each day for her letters, and to her visits from Montreal. As before, she was my extension into the everyday world, and could experience all that I could not. Lisa stunned me, and my first reaction was to try to do the same to her. But when I realized her confusion and torment, my goal became to help her. Lisa had given me so much, and I had given her little in return. I could try to hold her down, but how long would that satisfy my ego? It would not take Lisa long to realize that I was trying to control her, and her resentment would grow. I found myself in a difficult situation, and my lack of independence only aggravated it.

The only way I could hold onto Lisa was to loosen my grip. If she did not appreciate my actions today, she might at some point in the future. Then maybe, just maybe, I would have a chance. It was my only chance to maintain my relationship with her and to gain her respect. Without that respect, our relationship would be lost. Friendship was the basis of our love, and that friendship had rooted itself in trust and respect. Above all else, I wanted to maintain my friendship with Lisa.

It was not easy. My ego did not want to let go of whatever it still held. Lisa wanted something to get angry at me about, but something told me our time had come. It was time for a new level in our relationship.

"This would be so much easier if you were unreasonable with me!" she said. "Can't you give me something to hate you for?"

We agreed that Lisa would not drive the seven hours between Montreal and Gardiner every second weekend, as she had been doing. We would still talk on the phone and write letters, and we would always communicate honestly with one another. Montreal was her world to put in order herself. Both of us had a lot of rebuilding to do. I was satisfied. I could trust her to do what was best, and she valued that trust more than ever.

As my health improved, boredom became my major enemy. Boredom depressed me, and depression caused frustration. Many mornings I would sit in the bathtub and cry, not understanding what was happening to me. Much of my world was not as I had known it, and the crying gave me some release. Everyone was tugging at me, offering simple solutions to one or another of my many problems, wanting to make decisions for me. One day I wanted to wear a woolen vest I had gotten in India with Lisa two years earlier. The vest not only had sentimental value, but was also warm and comfortable.

"I think you should wear a sweater," my parents said.

"This vest is fine," I answered.

"We're just saying it for your own good. You will catch cold. Now go put on a sweater."

I blew up. "Jesus, I'm twenty-six years old! Don't you think I can make my own decisions?"

"I really think this once you ought to put on the sweater," my father continued.

"I've been on my own quite a while, you know," I said. "I've been around the world without you holding my hand."

"Go get a sweater!" my father said.

"Hold it," I said. "This issue isn't about whether I should wear a sweater; it's whether I have the right to make my own decision." I waited, hoping to draw them into an intense argument. They did not disagree, but they waited until I went to get my sweater.

Someone usually practiced walking outside with me three or four times a day. We lived on a quiet dead-end street with a flat, smooth surface that made it an excellent place for me to walk. The big problem was that we lived at the top of a hill, where the spring winds blew forcefully.

One day in May, I brought a cane home, and was eager to practice with it. A cane represented freedom, and I was ecstatic about reaching the point where I could use one. A walker was so bulky and cumbersome. I loved to feel the grain of the wood in my hand, and marveled at how easy it was to manage. With a cane, I thought, I can go back to school. I was on a roll and wanted to practice.

"Dad, let's go out and walk."

"I will in a minute," he said. "I want to finish this article first."

"I'll wait for you outside," I said.

For May, the day was cold and gray. When my father did not come out in minutes, I decided to start on my own. Walking with a cane was a new experience, and I liked it, but I was surprised at how little stability it allowed. I had to concentrate on each placement of the cane, each step I took.

I walked down to the pasture gate, two hundred feet away, and turned around using tiny steps. The front door looked a long way from where I stood, and as I looked up I almost lost my balance. Through the living room window, I could see my father reading in his chair.

I walked another thirty feet. A gust of wind raised a little dust in the road. I teetered, and then panicked. Instead of adjusting my balance, I anticipated the fall and looked for the best place to land on some soft spring grass. I waited for my father to look up from his paper, but he had just had a cataract operation and could not see me.

Unable to get up by myself, I had a problem. On an isolated dead-end road, no one saw that I needed help, and it was too cold to sit and wait. I could not even shout loud enough to call for help. My only choice seemed to be crawling to a telephone pole twenty feet away and trying to use the pole to pull myself up. I made my way to the pole, dragging my cane in tow, and wrapped my arms around it to hoist myself, but I was too tired even to get off my knees.

Fifteen minutes later, a city worker walked by and saw me kneeling in front of the telephone pole with my arms wrapped around it. Between fits of manic laughter, I managed to ask him for assistance. He must have thought I was crazy. Not until after I was standing did he force a smile. When I returned to the house, my father was still reading the newspaper, oblivious to the whole affair.

My vulnerability sometimes frightened me. A gust of wind, a crowd of people, or simply looking up would cause me to lose my balance. I did not want to be in a situation where I could fall and perhaps hurt myself seriously. I asked myself if I would be better off simply walking with a stable apparatus. Why be in such a hurry?

Then I remembered business school, my fight with boredom, and my desire for more freedom. Living at home with my parents was not ideal. The wild parties would have to wait. School was my best chance for an exit, and if I wanted to return to school in the fall, I had to push myself and take risks. How many of my classmates would have to worry about being blown over by a gust of wind?

Losing my balance and falling was only one of my fears. I would get up at night to go to the bathroom and not be clearheaded. Grabbing the walker beside my bed, I would hurry to the toilet. Reaching it was not a problem, but on the way back to my room I would break into a cold sweat. Almost without fail, I would experience sudden dizziness, faint, and collapse on the floor. At the sound of the thud, my mother would come running to find me in a sweat on the floor. My mother insisted I see a doctor about these spells, but I was afraid to discover the truth.

When I finally did visit the doctor, he told me it was vertigo caused by the pressure of urination. He warned me to sit up in bed for a few minutes before arising.

By the middle of May, I began weight training. In therapy, I practiced a military press with my cane. I strained to lift it above my head a second time, but my arms were too fatigued. I was never a weight lifter, but I'd never had trouble lifting a cane before, either.

By the end of the month, I managed to press three pounds. Arnold Schwarzenegger, here I come! I set a goal of a pound more a week, and would try to press eight pounds by the end of June. By the end of June, I surprised myself by lifting ten pounds above my head.

With guidance, I practiced walking around the Gardiner Common without my cane, with my father timing me as we walked. John and Nancy would be home the first of July to celebrate my father's 65th birthday, and one goal became being able to walk the quarter of a mile around the perimeter of the Common by then. At first, I could walk only one side of the square around the Common, but after three weeks of daily walks, I reached my goal of walking all four legs by the time they arrived home.

To combat boredom, I enrolled in a memory course at one of the local high schools, and an American History course at the University of Maine in Augusta. My memory proved to be as reliable as any of my classmates', but problems arose from my insecurities in dealing with others. Speaking spontaneously was not a problem, but when I thought about what I would say, I had trouble getting words out of my mouth. As my voice rose and quaked and my eyes watered, I would fight to maintain control. My frustration and embarrassment made it even more difficult. After one episode, I made sure to bring my cane to class the next week as a symbol of my malady. Graduate school loomed just two months ahead.

I failed my first History quiz. My first reaction was fear that perhaps I would not be able to compete. Everything I hoped to do was in jeopardy. What I feared most was the truth, often the most frightening discovery of all. I told myself that the quiz was not a good test of my abilities; it was a multiple-choice exam, with questions centered on unimportant facts and dates to make sure those students had done their reading carefully. I was not taking the course for credit, had not bought the book because I didn't want to spend the money, and had not done the reading.

Mental fatigue was a major barrier. In July, therapists determined through testing that my concentration level declined sharply after fifteen or twenty minutes. As I gazed out the window, the therapists doubted my ability to return to school, but I assured them that I had always been a dreamer who gazed out windows.

My real test would come when I drove to Boston and played a game of chess with my friend Andy. Andy was a bright opponent, but did not have much experience playing chess. He always provided an interesting challenge, but I had always prevailed against him. Playing chess with Andy would provide an accurate, if not scientific, gauge of my concentration ability. Before playing Andy, I had to drive to Boston. I smiled when I thought of that freedom.

My father took me to a factory parking lot in his bright red 1972 Plymouth Duster. Over the years the car had lost much of its maneuverability, and it floated from one side of the lane to the other. After three nights' practice, I announced that I was driving to Boston the next weekend.

The weekend arrived quickly. I had no trouble driving to Andy's house in Cambridge. We had our first game of chess on the morning I arrived. Although Andy had not played since our last game, he won easily.

"You caught me by surprise," I said. "I wasn't really ready."

"That's the first time I've beaten you," Andy laughed.

"You'd better take it while you can get it 'cause it'll never happen again," I said. "Savor it now, so you won't forget what it's like!"

The second game was much closer. I was constantly pressuring his king, but in hot pursuit I left an opening in my own defense, and Andy won again.

"This can't be happening," I said. "Maybe I'm just too impatient. I thought I had you trapped in that corner."

"I knew what I was doing all along," Andy said.

"Sure you did, you lucky bastard!"

That night we had a third game, and again I made Andy look like Bobby Fischer. "Three out of three? This can't be happening!"

I tried to make light of Andy's three consecutive victories, but I was the one using the chess matches to gauge my level of concentration. No matter how hard I tried to concentrate, I could not beat Andy, an opponent I had always beaten before. Maybe I was putting too much pressure on myself, but I could not quiet my mind and concentrate. It was the first time I had admitted to myself that my concentration was not good.

Everything was unsettled, but my heart was still set on going to school in less than two months. How could I improve my concentration level? I pretended that everything was proceeding as planned.

Lisa and I had an argument over the phone in early August. In a fit of rage, I told her our relationship was over for good. She wanted me to be the one to say it was over, but it was really a mutual decision. The events of the past year had strained our relationship beyond repair. What made our break bearable was my belief that after time, we would reunite.

"Come on, walk fast," my physical therapist urged. "What are you going to do when you have to cross the street in a hurry?"

Therapists dragged me by both shoulders, and my feet raced to keep up with them. They were preparing me for my attempt to return to school, and that day was rapidly approaching.

I cooked a spaghetti dinner in occupational therapy, and tried to foresee problems I might have living alone. Water in a pan was difficult for me to carry, but I would compensate. I practiced carrying books, but their weight upset my balance. I still could not walk downhill without falling, but Evanston was flat.

Psychologists came to my home to administer tests. "Eat little snacks high in protein throughout the day," they told me.

Fat chance, I thought.

On September 4th, two days before I left for school, my occupational therapist administered a final test. She had me copy two lines from a book, and timed me: two minutes and forty-five seconds. She copied the exact same lines in one minute and fifteen seconds.

"What are you going to do when you are taking notes?" she asked.

"I don't know, but I'll manage somehow," I said, feigning confidence. "I'll have to live with it." I wished everyone would leave me alone. I did not want to face the possibility of failure. I wasn't aware that the most difficult portions of my recovery were yet to come.

In September 1981, I returned to Northwestern's Kellogg Graduate School of Management .

## Chapter 14

# Alone in the Night

**B**efore heading to Chicago, I stopped in Washington, D.C. to visit some college friends, including Andy and Max. They had been an important support system during my illness, writing letters and speaking with Lisa on the phone.

The day after my arrival, Max, with whom I was staying, showed me around the city. It was a new and exciting look at D.C. Many things had changed since my last visit in 1971, and new government buildings had added a new silhouette to the skyline.

As a sixteen-year-old in 1971, I had traveled with a busload of other students to an anti-war demonstration. I had been one of nearly one million people from all over the country protesting American involvement in Vietnam. For a naïve sixteen-year-old from Maine, the sight of young men running in the streets of Washington D.C. and shouting, "Ho, Ho, homosexuals. Right on!" was a real learning experience.

That night, Max and I met Andy and a few other friends in a bar. My eyes followed the slightest movement, particularly movement by the girls wearing tight-fitting jeans. "They're not playing fair," I told my friends. After my relatively cloistered life with my parents in Maine, I was like a small boy let loose in a candy shop, but I avoided grabbing the merchandise. I felt a need to explain my situation in almost every conversation I started, as if I were apologizing. Never before had I had so much trouble communicating with Americans my own age.

As the night wore on, my friends scattered, leaving Max and me at the bar. Two girls were leaving at the same time as we did. In my infinite wisdom, I decided to meet them. I rubbed my eyes. "Will you help me find my contact?" I asked.

Max sighed and walked away in the opposite direction. "You haven't changed a bit," he slurred over his shoulder. "I'm going to get a cab; you can come if you want."

Of course, I did not go. I was having too much fun in the Washington night. The girls thought I was some kind of kook, but by then Max was out of sight. I waited hoping that somehow Max would be on the street, but I never saw him. I didn't mind—I was enjoying myself—but as I waited on the corner, the night grew cold and misty and I regretted my decision not to go with my friend.

A smile crossed my face. "That damn Max," I said aloud. Inside I was saying, "I'm alive!"

By 3:00 a.m., there was still no sign of Max and the bars had closed. I called his room, but got no answer. Max lived in the back of a house where he was house-sitting, and I did not see much hope of getting into his house if he wasn't there.

After another unsuccessful call at 3:30, I hailed a cab. Luckily, I remembered his address and had just enough cash to pay the driver. At the house, I found Max's car unlocked. I grabbed my jacket from it to cover myself against the wind and drizzle, and went around to the back of the house.

I looked through the window into his room. There he was, arms hanging off each side of the bed, passed out like a sleeping lion with not a care in the world. I knocked and shouted into the open window, but he did not stir. As the owners were in the house and it was wired for sound, I did not want to knock too loudly. After all, it was four thirty in the morning. My flight to Chicago left at 10:00 a.m.

I huddled on the cold cement stairs by Max's room, figuring I'd try to roust him periodically. I gathered my jacket against the cold night and said under my breath, "That damn Max."

As dawn approached, I finally roused him, and managed an hour's sleep before leaving for the airport. Both of us slouched in the front seat of his '73 steel blue Pontiac station wagon. What I would do for a couple hours of sleep, I thought. Damn, I could kick myself in the butt. We wore sunglasses, but still squinted straight ahead. Neither of us uttered a word, lest we jar our brains.

Max left me standing alone—really alone for the first time since the previous fall, when I had gone into a coma. I wasn't frightened, but eager to meet the world head-on. I was ready for the jabs; I only hoped I could ward off the knockout punches.

I had not given much thought as to why I wanted to return to business school, but that had been my goal while lying locked-in nearly a year earlier. It was not a matter of determination; it was a matter of expectation. I expected to return to graduate school at Northwestern University, and I was never willing to hear otherwise. I knew that I'd have to push myself. I never believed it would be easy, but neither did I realize how difficult it would be.

My mind was atrophying as I walked around the Common, lap after lap. I needed to be stimulated both mentally and physically. Finding a job in a small town during the recession would be next to impossible, and I doubted that any other school would offer me as generous a financial aid package. I had reliable friends in Evanston, friends I would need. Northwestern offered entry only in the fall. If I did not enroll this fall, I would have to wait another entire year, and I didn't have that time to lose. I'd be damned if anyone was going to tell me I could not do it.

I felt a great sense of freedom in finally being on my own, with my own apartment, my own kitchen, and my own alarm clock. The sense of freedom faded quickly as my apartment mate arrived, a twenty-one-year-old Greek Canadian who was as different from me as salt is from pepper. Studies came easily to him; they had always been difficult for me. He was immature, short and stout, and always ran wherever he went. I prided myself on being street smart; I could handle myself in a variety of situations. Compared with him, I was experienced in terms of years and miles traveled. I was lean and lanky and moved methodically.

What had always come easily to me, I found most difficult in those first days. I had trouble reacting and talking with people. My self-confidence was at an all-time low, and others could sense my insecurity. These people had no way of knowing who I was; I could not expect them to understand me.

I had been living in a bubble. I had lived in a stale environment for nearly a year, where my only daily contact was with therapists, family, and a few others who were aware of what had happened to me. Now the bubble had burst, and I was on my own. I was thrown into a group of competitive, bright people, and a struggle I had only dreamed of had begun. For the first time, I realized that the dream could easily become a nightmare.

I searched for a symbol of my malady, but found none. I had had my cane or my trusty urinal with me for months, but now I was naked against the cold. People had always treated me well when I walked with a cane; they held doors open, and often nodded and smiled. I had joked that even when I no longer needed the cane, I would still walk with it because others would hold doors open and smile. In the fall of 1981, it was no joke.

I had always made friends easily, but now I felt like an outsider. People shied away, and I could not understand exactly why. Classmates would exchange a few pleasantries, and then vanish, leaving me alone with my thoughts. I always placed the blame on myself for acting odd. I needed friends; I felt very alone.

During the first term, it was easier for me to associate with second-year students, even though our schedules were very different. Second-year students were not only more comfortable in the surroundings, but many also knew me from the previous year, before I had become ill. They were better able to understand my recent history and current situation.

In the first term, the class of 350 students was divided into seven sections of approximately fifty students each. Sam had been in my original section, and was now a second-year student. That section had received daily reports on my condition during my hospital stay, and it was the students of that section with whom I felt the most comfortable.

Accounting would be the most difficult subject, and the one that would require the most time. Over the past year, my mind had become undisciplined and disorganized. My greatest concern was learning the concepts, not organizing the exact numbers in their places. *After all,* I told myself, *I am not learning to become an accountant.*

Nevertheless, Accounting was part of the program. In order to stay in school, I had to abide by the rules, even when I did not agree with those rules. I had weighed my alternatives and chosen this one. One of the requirements of this alternative was Accounting.

My whole being was concerned with the ability to perform as I would have a year earlier, even if it meant failing in school. I needed to prove to myself that I could scrape and scramble and struggle over hurdles. Only then would I know I had completed my odyssey and regained my old self.

My classmates were always in a hurry to get to class, to the library, to study. Although I, too, went everywhere at my top speed, I provided a sharp contrast to them. I could only walk slowly, and early in the fall I was only writing at half-speed. Discussing this with my former neurologist helped me to accept the problem. I always underestimated the time it would take to complete activities. He understood, and pointed out that even everyday activities like eating, showering, or going to the bathroom required more time.

After walking from my apartment to the school, a distance of approximately three-tenths of a mile, I had to sit and rest. The walk to school became a much-needed time to relax. I could not help thinking that other harried classmates would do well to take a few minutes to relax and breathe some fresh air. The fall was a pleasant one, but my classmates had no time to realize it; they were too busy struggling with their own problems and insecurities. Like me, they were trying to get a fix on business school. Their problems were not much different from my own. Time, for example, was a limited resource for us all. Each of us was involved in our own world with our own barriers to overcome.

As my classmates hurried past me, I was sometimes disappointed that they did not slow down and walk along with me. "Settle down, don't be in such a hurry," I wanted to tell them. "Check out the leaves on this tree."

"Come on, Mark, can't you walk any faster?" they urged.

"You go on ahead," I said.

"I've got to run to the bookstore before class," and they would be off. All my classmates were extremely busy during the fall, and as they rushed by, I was left thinking about what was most important to me.

One sunny, unusually warm day, as the leaves were just starting to fall, I stopped to watch some of the undergraduates play Frisbee. The flying Frisbee, the warmth of the sun, and the breeze on my face brought back memories of a day in the Philippines.

Lisa and I had been standing on the bow of a barca, a type of motorized outrigger canoe. The bright sun of the early morning seemed to glide across the water as it rose and revealed the colorful coral shimmering white, pink, and red beneath the surface of the water. As the barca increased its speed, the breeze was refreshing and alive. I saw a school of flying fish jump from the water and fly through the air. Their flight was not a smooth, graceful one; they danced and dipped like the flight of the Frisbee. The flying fish had to struggle to remain airborne, but their freedom, although brief, made my spirits soar. Not only did they have the vast ocean to play in, but unlike other fish, they could fly above it.

The flying Frisbee reminded me of that freedom, a freedom that I envied.

In the early weeks of fall, I did not make the time to exercise. Exercise had been my primary concern just a month earlier, but now I barely had time to think about it. My sense of guilt for not taking the time was outweighed by my difficulties with my studies. I had to settle for the walk to and from school as my exercise for the day.

I concentrated on three important elements of my well-being and survival: relating to others, trying to maintain my health and stress level, and keeping everything in clear perspective. I had no magic formula for relating with others except the knowledge that I had had success in the past. I tried to understand them and to be sensitive to their needs.

It was essential for me to handle stress and maintain my health. Unless I handled stress effectively, my health would be worse than before I matriculated at Northwestern. Even under the best of circumstances, I was in a very stressful situation, and I lacked the time and energy to combat that stress with many of the usual methods. I could not, for example, relieve my stress with vigorous exercise.

I began the day by eating a good breakfast, and concentrated on eating three regular meals a day. The time spent preparing meals, although short, became an important time to relax. I also felt that a good night's sleep was important to maintaining my health, even if my studies suffered.

My secret fear was a relapse. Whenever the thought arose, I would try to put it out of my mind as quickly as it had entered. The probability of a relapse was not high, but as long as the possibility existed, I was going to get my sleep no matter what.

My greatest challenge was keeping everything in perspective, with professors and classmates fueling constant pressure. The massive overload of material pulled me in several different directions. Balancing my health with my studies was only one area where I had to make tradeoffs—tradeoffs that made me feel unsure and insecure. My studies were teetering on the edge of disaster. They were important, but I had to decide where their importance ended. I had to gamble to survive, and it was on people that I decided to wager my future.

I called Lisa two or three times a week. She was trying to adjust to her own new world, but she was always willing to talk and listen.

"Stop making excuses," she told me. "I know you can do it, and so do you."

"I know I can. I know I can," I said. "That's why it is so frustrating."

I could never judge how much I could do; I always thought I could do more or better. Not judging accurately was frightening, and I became very insecure.

I tried to be a "good" student, organizing my time well. I would study both Friday and Saturday nights, something I had never done before, and I would wake at 5:00 a.m. to study in the morning before class. Why was I punishing myself? Life had not always been such a struggle, and there was no reason why it should be now. On Saturday nights, I wondered what I was doing in a study room with no windows, only fluorescent lights to keep me company.

As it often did, my mind traveled to exciting faraway lands. I remembered Christmas Eve in Chiang Mai, Thailand, two years earlier. Preparing for a romantic evening with Lisa and a bottle of champagne we had carried all the way from Hong Kong, I lit what I thought was a candle in front of the Christmas tree we had decorated. Sparks illuminated the room, and I went diving for cover, screaming "Fire! Fire!" Like an ostrich burying its head in the sand against a sand storm, I hid beneath a sheet as sparks filled the room. The innkeeper came to my rescue and explained that the candle was actually a sparkler.

Going to see my teachers during the fall was difficult. I had trouble maintaining my composure, and each experience attacked my ego. My voice would quake and my eyes would water. A cold shiver would run the length of my spine and rattle my whole body, but I had to get out what I was planning to say. I would lose my breath as if I were sobbing. I felt like cowering in a corner or being comforted in Lisa's caring arms. The more I concentrated on what I wanted to say, the more difficult it became.

The changes were not all negative. I was improving dramatically, not only physically but mentally as well. Each day I walked to class a little faster and wrote more clearly. With each class I could sense my mind becoming more finely tuned. The excitement of the dramatic changes forced me to push myself harder and harder. I could see that my effort was worthwhile, and I was gaining confidence and growing more secure.

Four weeks into the fall term, everything was proceeding smoothly—too smoothly. "Business school isn't as tough as they say," I thought. "I can handle this. This is where I belong."

Midterms came, and my problems started in earnest. By the luck of the draw, my section was scheduled for three midterms and a long paper, all due on two consecutive days. I asked for and received an extension on the paper. The professor, Liam Fahey, understood my predicament and was aware of my condition. He wished me luck.

Tension mounted as the first day of exams neared. Conversation in the library centered on how little sleep everyone had gotten. The coffee machine in the library lounge was a favorite gathering spot. The first day featured Accounting at nine in the morning, followed by an Organizational Behavior exam after lunch.

I awoke the morning of the Accounting exam and remained calm as I ate breakfast and showered. If I became tense, as many of my classmates were, I would be lost. As soon as I entered the room where the exam was being held, I could sense the pressure mounting. My classmates were nervous, jittery, and anxious. Chatter in the room was deafening.

"Hope she doesn't ask any questions on Chapter 3, because I didn't get much chance to review that," I heard someone say.

"How did that go again?" the girl in the corner asked her neighbor.

"Hope she oversleeps and doesn't show."

"This is only an exam," I repeated to myself. "Get a hold of yourself."

The pressure just kept mounting and mounting and mounting until the professor handed out the exams. Her eyes purposely did not meet mine as she laid a test booklet on my desk. Pencils tapping sounded like cannon fire, and people squirming in their seats distracted me. My head jerked uncontrollably to the right and my teeth started to grind. Cold shivers ran up my spine, but I tried to remain in control.

"You can do it," I told myself. "Get it together."

I read over the exam while my Accounting professor pranced around the room. I felt as if she was waiting for me to fail, not even expecting that I could do it. And the worst part of it was, I could not.

# Chapter 15

# Breaking Point

If I had remained calm in the Accounting exam, I could have finished it, but I panicked. In college I'd prided myself on maintaining my composure and being at an emotional peak during an exam. I might not have known the material as well as some, but I knew how to prepare myself. The second night before an exam I would have a glass of wine, relax, and get a full night's rest without the anxiety of the approaching test. With a good sleep behind me, I was able to devote more effort to studying and not be as concerned with getting sleep as I would have been had I not relaxed the previous night. Instead of studying late into the night, I liked to wake early in the morning after four or five hours' sleep, when there were less disturbances.

I always stopped studying an hour before an exam, no matter how well I knew the material, to take a shower. Then I would return to my room and play loud, inspiring music, like Bruce Springsteen or Ronnie Laws, to prepare myself psychologically for the upcoming ordeal. This formula was not always effective, but even if I did not do as well as I had expected, I would be in much better mental condition to deal with the results than many of my frazzled friends.

That fall term I was trying to be a "good" student, and was afraid to try the approach that had gotten me through university and to Northwestern. Instead of concentrating on relaxing and thinking about the exam, I thought of ways out: out of the room, out of Accounting and maybe even out of school. Before the first five minutes of the test had passed, I had already thought of dropping Accounting.

*I know, I'll drop a course or two and go to night school!* I assured myself. *School is too tough for me right now! I'm crazy to even think about th*is. I searched for ways to leave the room. Should I hand in my paper now in front of the whole class, or should I wait until the end of class when I can inconspicuously hand it in with others? The teacher was standing at the head of the class, her arms folded, surveying the room. She must have noticed that I was not writing. Everyone else seemed to be writing furiously.

"What am I doing here?" I wanted to shout, but the silence of others restrained me. *What's pushing me to torture myself? I sure don't want to be here right now.*

I felt self-conscious as I stood, walked in front of the class, and handed in a blank test paper. Not wanting to admit defeat, I avoided the professor's eyes.

As I went to Dean Wilson's office, a demon inside me tried to escape. I feared my own skin could not contain it. I went to the Dean's office, not because of the position he held, but because I needed someone with whom to talk. I was seeking sanctuary. I trusted and respected the Dean; he had become my best friend in Evanston.

My voice quaked uncontrollably as I asked his secretary if he was available. Its pitch rose as I struggled to regulate the airflow. My eyes watered as I tried to release words from my mouth, but at the same time I was trying to restrain the demon. I did not understand what was happening to me. I was filled with self-doubt and nearing my breaking point. It was a relief to find him available.

I told him what had happened in Accounting, how I panicked. I searched for excuses, but none of them satisfied me. Nothing sounded right. I could not put into words how I felt, but my trembling voice and watery eyes revealed a serious problem. Doubts surfaced about continuing school another day, another hour.

Although he remained calm on the outside, I could tell from his expression that the Dean was not sure I could continue, either. "The first thing to do is relax. Don't judge everything on this one test. Don't be so quick to judge yourself," he told me.

I started to control my voice, but the morning's events did not want to settle down quickly, and my voice still quaked. Its pitch rose again, and I had to wait before I continued to speak.

"If you think it's beyond your capabilities, then you definitely shouldn't be in school," he said. "But what are you going to do—return to Gardiner and walk around the Common every day?"

I looked at the floor and thought, *if I can't do this, what can I do?* I was afraid to face the truth. I had thought too long about this option, and excluded other ones. I could not see beyond failure at this point. *Where will I go? What can I do now?* My world had changed.

Dean Wilson is right, I thought, trying to compose myself. I can't judge myself on one Accounting exam. Even if I can't make it in school, I'm no failure. In the pressure of an intense academic situation, it was difficult to see beyond the school's boundaries.

I decided to take my Organizational Behavior exam that afternoon before making any decisions. The Organizational Behavior exam was a case analysis—an essay exam that was more like the exams I had taken as a History major in college.

My mind drifted to a time in India when a solution to my problem had arisen from the depths of chaos and despair. My sister and Dana had gone to the Golden Temple in Amritsar. I had not felt energetic, and had volunteered to buy the train tickets to Delhi. After I bought the tickets, I went out onto the train platform, and was surprised to find throngs of people, many of whom seemed to have settled down and taken permanent lodging in the station. It was apparent that we would not have an easy time getting on the train.

"We have to get to Delhi," I said aloud. A friend of ours was waiting for us in Delhi with some of our belongings, and he was scheduled to leave Delhi in less than two days. The train to Delhi took twelve to fifteen hours.

I asked an Indian gentleman who I thought might speak English if there was any problem getting on the train to Delhi.

"Of course, there is always a problem getting on a train to Delhi," the Indian answered in a melodic voice, and with a tilt of the head unique to Indians.

I had only been in India for a few hours, but I had already had enough. It was too chaotic, and I wanted to leave. Returning to Pakistan was impossible, but I was not about to stay here with its teeming swarms. Our only alternative seemed to be moving on to Delhi.

"See these people?" the Indian gentleman continued. "Some of them have been waiting here for days. The train will roll in and all the windows will be locked. As the windows are opened, it is each man for himself."

I looked around at the agile Indians, and my heart sank even lower. In Pakistan, I had jumped through an open train window as it pulled into the station in order to get adjoining seats for the three of us, but the platform was not nearly as crowded as this. In Pakistan, Nancy and Dana had had time to pass our belongings through the window.

*I just can't deal with any more hassles*, I thought. *This is nuts!*

The day had started in Lahore, Pakistan, with the discovery that our camera had been stolen by the owners of the inn where we were staying. After an intense argument, they finally gave it back, but our eagerness to flee the scene caused us to miss breakfast. On our way to the Indian border, I was body-searched by men who claimed to be plainclothes policemen and said that they were searching for drugs. Their badges were official-looking, but I had no way of understanding what was written on them. I had little choice but to believe them, and then I did not know if they wanted to fill their quota or collect some payoff money. I always carried a small amount of U.S. currency in case of a need to make a payoff.

Once they searched me and found that I was clean, they had a discussion amongst themselves. Finally, they allowed me to go free, but not until they had made me sweat. Later, at the only open border crossing between India and Pakistan, my sister had been strip-searched, and Dana and I had been questioned about Pakistani troop movement. After an arduous bus trip into the city of Amritsar, I was left on my own to decide what our next step would be, and to make matters even worse, I was not feeling well. I knew I had to remain calm. How would an Indian deal with this problem?

The crowd swelled in anticipation of the train's arrival. When Nancy and Dana finally joined me, I told them, "We won't make it. This is a madhouse, you wouldn't believe it!" Nancy and Dana both looked distraught. "I can't put up with this anymore."

"OK, but we've got to make it to Delhi," Nancy said. "Bob's leaving the day after tomorrow if we don't show."

Three porters approached us with a solution to our problem. "For five rupees each, we will get you sleepers," they said in broken English.

We did not believe them, especially when they insisted we pay them first. Finally deciding that the risk was worth taking, we were shocked at our good fortune. We haggled them down to four rupees each (the equivalent of about fifty cents). We would gladly have paid them each five rupees, but we had to save face! Although we still had to fight the crowd and the bedlam, we made it to Delhi the next day and met Bob.

Now, sitting in the Dean's office, I waited for a solution to rescue me.

Dean Wilson was my friend and counselor in the fall of 1981. He was my anchor in the rough sea, knowing my problem better than anyone. He was familiar with the roots of my issues, and the territory where the school and I crossed paths, territory that was foreign to me.

I felt much better after taking my Organizational Behavior exam that afternoon and my Linear Programming exam the next morning, but a serious problem developed. The management paper on which I had gotten the extension was a group paper. We had been working as a group all semester and it was a major focus of the class. Besides me, the group comprised four other students. I should have given the group top priority, and gotten an extension on the Accounting exam instead. All term I had been struggling to keep up with the group and to provide an equal share. I could not accurately judge how much I could contribute. Other members of the group tried to help, but their frustration was apparent, and when I did have something to contribute, I was not very persuasive.

The group spent many hours together without me, preparing for the midterm paper, and everything had gone smoothly. After the paper, a closeness developed among the four, and they decided that they functioned better without me. They were not going to let me back into the group. Not only would I have to do the midterm paper on my own, but I would have to prepare the daily class material outside the group, and group discussion was an important part of class. It was devastating. I didn't see how I could continue in school.

It was not even the class workload that disturbed me the most. Somehow I would manage; it was the feeling that classmates abandoned me because I was struggling harder than they were. I tried and wanted to contribute an equal share, but I had not held up my end. Sometimes you chase the bus and you just don't catch it. In fairness to the other group members, they did try to help me judge how much I could do. They had their problems; they did not have time for mine. Under the circumstances, I was on my own. They had set their priorities, and I was too much of a burden to carry. I felt burdensome.

The experience staggered me. I had put so much faith in people, but

I did not carry my share. I was stunned, finished, and ready to fall to the canvas. I awaited the referee's count: ten…nine…eight. What had I been thinking? This wasn't Afghanistan or the Philippines or Little League. I was playing with the big boys. How could I have made such a miscalculation? This was one of the top graduate business schools in the country, not summer camp. I had failed to adapt to the situation, and had underestimated what I needed to do in order to survive. I had focused on my goals and aspirations without factoring my environment into the equation.

I learned a valuable lesson. The experience hardened me, and I only hoped that the other group members learned as much about group dynamics and setting priorities that fall term as I did.

When the Dean suggested that maybe I should see a psychiatrist, I was indignant. I had had enough of doctors giving me answers. It was time I searched for some of my own.

When I expressed this indignation to my mother one night during a phone conversation, she surprised me by saying, "Maybe you should." The shock made me give more serious consideration to the idea, but I quickly dismissed the thought. It would have been a long and costly ordeal for a psychiatrist simply to understand my problem, and I had neither time nor money to spare. I could not put my problem into words. It was too complex for me to understand the problem, let alone propose a solution. I was accustomed to solving my own problems. I did not feel comfortable voicing them to others, and I did not need a sympathetic ear telling me to put my life on hold or that it was all right if I failed. I needed to be pushed. I would find a solution. Visiting a psychiatrist would only frustrate me more, and I feared what he might say.

My mind drifted to a freer time without any unpleasant classes.

Nancy, Dana, and I had been traveling with a British couple that we had just met the day before. We were all traveling from Kandahar, Afghanistan to a village to get a bus to Quetta, Pakistan. We had just had our visas checked outside the village, and in order to get to the bus we had to hire some motorized tri-shaws. Nancy, Dana, and I haggled with the driver of one, and he agreed to take us to the village. The price was more than we expected to pay, and we were very tired after traveling all day. The British couple took another tri-shaw, and planned to meet us at the bus.

We arrived first, placed our belongings on top of sacks of grain in the back of the bus, and waited for the British couple, John and Anne. Ten minutes later they arrived, arguing with the driver of the tri-shaw. The argument was getting heated and attracting a crowd of perhaps thirty to forty people. As the argument grew more intense, the five of us got into the back of the bus, with John continuing the argument at the back door. The villagers began picking up stones.

I could see us getting stoned to death in some remote village in Pakistan where authority seemed nonexistent. We questioned John about the disturbance. He explained to us, while still arguing with the driver, that they had not agreed upon a price before their ride, and now the driver wanted an outlandish amount of money. The driver grabbed for John's watch and tried to rip it from his wrist, breaking the skin in the process. The crowd was becoming more agitated, and John was losing his temper. The bus driver started the engine and drove off before a more serious outbreak developed.

This was all because John had not agreed on a mutually acceptable price before the tri-shaw ride. It could have been a disastrous situation, but I learned from it.

*Had I been learning more back then?* I wondered. *If I have a degree, what does it prove? My doubts about returning to school continued, but I always came back to the same question: What is my best alternative?*

*If I dropped a class now,* I asked myself, *would that just be a crutch?*

Dropping a class would weaken my whole strategy, I thought. Once I started looking for ways to escape my problem, a landslide might occur, and I would drop more classes whenever I found myself in trouble. The next term I had to take Statistics and Managerial Economics, two courses where I would have more problems. If I had to take five courses in one term I would be in deeper trouble, because there was no way I could see myself withstanding the pressure of five courses.

I was looking for a way out of the mess. Was what I was trying to do fair to me, to the school, to Dean Wilson or to the students in my group? It was a challenge to hold myself together and not break down, a problem I had never experienced before.

My problem was more than just school. School was secondary. It was my being, my self-respect. I was unsure that I could handle the challenge. All I knew was that I was trembling and crying uncontrollably.

After midterms, each section of fifty students received money to have a party for that section. The night of our party was the first night out since the beginning of classes six weeks earlier for most of us, and we all needed a release.

Our section decided to have our party in a rented function room on Rush Street. Rush Street was an area lined with bars catering to all types, and packed with people barhopping from one saloon to the next. Some of the best jazz and blues bars in the country were on the fringes of Rush Street, along with piano bars and strip shows. Rush Street was a much-needed respite from the windowless walls of the study rooms and the library coffee machine.

The section party was subdued and relaxing. We all enjoyed a chance to drink, talk, and forget about our individual worries. Still, it was difficult to steer a conversation away from school. As the night wore on, the section broke into smaller groups. Although I was welcomed to join various groups, I found myself drifting off alone.

I wandered to other bars, where I watched people with curiosity. My face had a puzzled expression as I looked at the crowd as if under a large magnifying glass. I had seen it all before, and yet it was somehow all new to me. I wanted to be a part of the dancing, partying, and conversation, but only looked on, not knowing how to relate and feeling as if I did not belong.

After the bars closed, I wandered the streets of Chicago, but I was not sure about the object of my search. Was it life on a park bench? Was it a girl, or whether I belonged in school?

Walking down Michigan Avenue, the fashionable street in downtown Chicago, I passed the fifty-plus stories of the John Hancock Center and the Fire Tower, the only building left standing in the area after the Great Chicago Fire nearly one hundred years earlier.

A hooker approached me. It was late, and most of her customers had gone home long ago. She tried to seduce me with an affordable price. After giving it some serious thought, I turned her down.

"Well, I thought I'd try," she said. "It looked like you were searching for something." Her eyes were tender for a lady of the street, and I longed for some comforting arms to embrace me and assure me that everything would be fine. What could I tell her I was searching for? I did not even know myself. I wanted to know the answers, but I did not even know the questions.

"Thanks for the offer," I said, "but I guess not tonight."

We parted ways, and my search continued. I was staggering a great deal. The few people I passed thought I was drunk, but it was just that my legs were very weak. I stopped along the way and rested on park benches where I could find a spot among the homeless drunks.

As the sun rose, I took the train back to Evanston, still not having found any answers to my problem. I returned to my world of accounting and linear programming.

Was there any place for me in the business world? Was I just a lead weight, I wondered, slowing the progress of my fellow students? I was walking a tightrope, and the tightrope was swaying in the wind. With just one slip I would plunge to the earth far below. In college, my freshman English professor had warned my class that we would all become jugglers, juggling as many bowling pins as we could until one critical day when they all might fall, and we had to be prepared for that day. I was juggling on a swaying tightrope, too preoccupied to prepare myself for a fall.

During that first term, I felt I was learning everything for the first time. Things that seemed obvious to others were unclear to me. But along with relearning how to walk and write and how to relate with people, I was regaining an important sense of self. With my new self-awareness, I was beginning to feel that when my ordeal was over, I would be stronger than ever. I was the best judge of my actions, and if I could not live up to everyone's expectations, I could live up to my own.

With increased self-awareness, I began to understand the battles of those around me. Immersed in self-doubt, I realized that Kate, one of the top students in my section, was also struggling. In her late twenties, she was a captive of her own competitive nature and her fear of the unknown. She struggled with her desire to have children and her desire to have a career. She saw herself as a human time bomb ticking away until the day when it would be too late. As her career developed, she would move further and further away from her dream of having children. Kate saw herself competing with men on equal grounds; she did not want employers pre-judging her just because she was a woman, and yet at the same time, she did want a child. I saw that her struggle was more serious than my own.

Then there was Joe, a Jesuit priest in his mid-thirties, another fellow student whom I watched with great interest. Joe had not been a student for several years, serving six years as the successful headmaster of a parochial high school on Chicago's Southside. As a young headmaster, he had reversed the school's downward trend and restored its reputation as a top school. Joe had loved what he was doing, but his Jesuit supervisor felt that he needed a less stressful job because of a heart condition, and ordered him from his post.

Like me, Joe was experiencing problems with Accounting and Linear Programming. He was out of the habits of studying and taking tests. Joe was well-liked, respected, and valuable to our classmates because he kept everything in perspective. He was struggling with health problems—a heart condition that doctors had difficulty controlling. I admired the way Joe always found time to laugh at himself despite his problems, and saw that he was valuable to our fellow students. His example helped me to remain calm and to see my own strengths and limitations.

I often ate dinner at a local restaurant, and I had become friendly with one of the waitresses who worked there. One night the pressure of school became unbearable; I was tired of my cloistered lifestyle. I asked the waitress, Christie, to dinner for the next night. With a little persuasion, she accepted.

It was refreshing to spend time away from campus with an earthy and vivacious young woman who talked intelligently about subjects other than grades or professors. School was so consuming that it was next to impossible to relax completely with a fellow student. Unlike the faces of many of my classmates, Christie's face was not all tense.

Christie was the first person with whom I was able to spend time without finding it necessary to explain my medical history. I had always felt awkward and self-conscious with others until they knew the source of my problems. Instead of judging myself on my own merits, I was continually comparing myself with others.

Everything was proceeding fine until I tripped over a miniscule crack in the sidewalk on the way to the restaurant. Stumbling to the ground, I fell flat as a fallen tree. I was unhurt, but with the sudden jar, I once again felt insecure, and my neck jerked involuntarily. If I had been relaxed, I could have put Christie at ease, but awkwardly I tried to explain how my medical history affected my every move. It was as difficult for her to understand as it was for me to explain. From the moment I tripped over the crack, my relationship with Christie was never the same, but the relationship marked a new stage in dealing with people. No longer did I feel I had to explain my actions or my every move.

As I grew more self-confident and aware, I realized that what I was learning at Northwestern was far more important than what I would have been learning walking laps around the Common at home, and I set my resolve to stay. Although my classes remained important, what I was learning outside the classroom was more so. I had to reset my priorities accordingly. My ego had been shattered during my midterms, and it was difficult to bounce back for another exam.

My Accounting professor allowed me to retake my midterm in a private room without the distractions of other students. I received a D+. I had not done well on the test by the professor's standards, but I had scored well enough by my own. I wanted to be in the range of other students on the first test, and I had managed to score better than some. The Accounting professor was surprised to discover that I was as satisfied with my score as most students were when they received an A.

Linear Programming still gave me trouble, but I was satisfied that I was managing the best I could under the circumstances. Without a group in management, I was at least tagging along. The professor, Liam Fahey, was not only a great professor, but a great man as well. He helped me put my situation in perspective.

The faculty sensed my struggle. They were always available to help me solve my problems and review areas that I did not understand. For the most part, students were the ones who created the tense, competitive environment. The faculty provided a calm learning setting. I often found it easier to talk with professors than I did with other students. Luckily, Kellogg was and is a school that promotes well-rounded individuals, and not solely great students.

The challenge of the first term, with its tests and papers, illuminated new priorities. I was learning how important others were to my well-being, which I had never understood before. At Northwestern, I was learning more than simple tests or papers could measure; I was refining my ability to establish priorities and relearning how to relate to others outside of a hospital environment.

Snow arrived, and with the snow came my finals. I did not have time to see the spectacular Christmas lights in downtown Chicago. All I wanted was to return to Maine; I was drained of emotion. I went through the motions and hoped for favorable results.

I struggled all night to type a paper that was my last assignment of the term, and finally handed it in at ten o'clock in the morning. The sun shone brightly in the clear sky, bouncing off the four inches of new snow that had fallen the night before. On the walk back to my apartment, the snow crunched beneath my feet, and the cold air refreshed my tired eyes.

When the thought struck, my eyes watered and my body reverberated with joy. "I've made it!" I shouted in disbelief. I had proven to myself that I was back. A long journey still lay ahead of me, but at least I was traveling the right road.

## Chapter 16

# Moving On

I graduated from the Kellogg Graduate School of Management at Northwestern University in June 1983. When Dean Wilson announced my name, I walked awkwardly across the stage. Although I could walk quickly when necessary, my legs were still stiff, and it was necessary for me to concentrate to walk a straight line.

As I received my diploma, I was particularly honored to see my Accounting professor stand and applaud. More than ever, I realized that without support from many people, I never would have graduated. With watery eyes, I fought to maintain control of my emotions and contain the ball of energy within me. Conscious of each step, the walk seemed endless, but at last I descended the stairs into my brother's congratulating arms.

Graduate school had been an extremely difficult path. It was part of my re-entry into a normal life, and I was thankful that it was behind me. The first term I had skimmed by with two Bs and two Ds, barely managing the C average that was necessary to stay in the program. In my second term, Statistics and Managerial Economics had proved to be too much, and I was forced to drop one course and take an "Incomplete" in another. By the summer of 1982, I was ready for a vacation, and found myself trying to decide what I was going to do with my future. After finishing the fall term of my second year, I was burned out and emotionally drained. Unsure what I was going to do, I was rapidly losing interest in school. My main goal was to graduate. Learning became secondary.

More than two hundred recruiters from large corporations came to the business school during the early months of 1983 to interview prospective hires. Most of the first interviews were a half-hour in length, conducted in small windowless rooms. The jobs in question were responsible, well-paying positions, and companies spared no expense to attract well-qualified candidates. In the weeks that followed the first interviews, successful interviewees flew to other cities around the country for a round of second interviews at the corporations' main headquarters. It was a high-pressure situation for all candidates.

I spent hours in practice situations with counselors and video cameras to prepare for interviewing. My problems stemmed from the lingering slur in my speech, a voice that quaked in tense situations, and a nervous, uncontrollable giggle and mannerisms, such as covering my mouth with my hand when insecure. I practiced answers to various questions that might arise and tried not to sound scripted. By the time recruiters came to the school, both my counselor and I were confident in my interviewing ability.

My medical history continued to be an issue. I could almost pass without mentioning it, but my resume had a year-long gap, and it was sure to arise in the course of a half-hour interview. My first counselor thought it would be best to downplay my history as much as possible, not even mentioning my recent medical history unless it became absolutely necessary. His approach for me was to back into a job by looking like everyone else and not making any mistakes. Perhaps he was right, but that was not my way. I was not going to hide my past.

I thought that the past two years demonstrated a great management experience, and I was sure someone would see it my way. After all, "challenge" was a word recruiters liked to use. What greater challenge could people my age cite? It demonstrated that I could set goals and was action-oriented. My formal education was strong. My work experience and my trips to Asia, which I had paid for myself, showed initiative. I was ready to move forward, and liked the new challenge.

A thirty-second statement concerning the gap in my resume at the beginning of the interview would not only answer many questions, but would also be a way of asserting myself early in the interview. I hoped it would get the interview off to a fast start, but the interviews did not move in the right direction. The problem was that the interviewers always had questions about my illness, and in the half-hour meetings, little time remained to discuss other areas of mutual concern.

In the first three interviews, problems with my voice led to insecurity. I chalked the interviews up to experience, but I was pleasantly surprised when one of the corporations invited me to Minneapolis for a second meeting, a series of six forty-five minute interviews that comprised an exhausting day. Unfortunately, the trip did not result in a job offer.

Before graduation I had approximately forty interviews, but only one other resulted in a second meeting, this one in New York City. Interviewers did not know how to react to me. They were impressed by my accomplishments, but they did not readily apply them to business situations no matter how I tried to make the connection. My medical history gave them a solid reason to cross my name off their list of prospective candidates, all of whom were well-qualified. All but a handful of my classmates had accepted a job offer by graduation, and others accepted offers shortly after. I was just one step away from a job offer, but that step was a giant one.

I stayed in Chicago after graduation to look for a job because I would have a wider range of opportunities there than in Maine. By the end of July, the pressure of finding a job increased, my expectations decreased, and a lack of money forced me home. The due date for my school loans was approaching, and I saw no hope in sight. Frustrated, I returned to Maine.

Once home, my outlook about finding a job improved. I liked Portland, and was eager to get a job in that area. I renewed contact with my social worker, and she helped me enter a program in Portland that was designed to help handicapped persons of all types find jobs. I felt confident that the program would benefit me; it had several contacts in the Maine business community. I worked hard and interviewed with several companies.

The problem of how to address my medical history was still unresolved, making the search more difficult. At this point, I tried to downplay it as much as possible, but it always came up in the conversation. It usually changed the mood of the interview, raising many more questions than it answered. I became insecure, and knew they saw me as a risky candidate.

At times, I would feel frustrated and low, but overall I surprised myself with my positive outlook. I was eager to get a meaningful, responsible job because I had a lot to give, and I wanted the money that would enable me to live on my own.

It took me a long time to realize the difficulties for an applicant who has the stigma of being disabled. Employers have little reason to take a risk when other well-qualified candidates are available. They are willing to fill quotas by hiring disabled persons to fill low-level positions, such as mail delivery or maintenance workers, but they are often unwilling to give higher-paid, responsible jobs to someone who does not fit their mold. The more jobs for which I interviewed, the more questions were raised as to where I would be most comfortable.

I was excited by the prospects of many jobs, but I was afraid that my feeling of not knowing exactly where I belonged was apparent to everyone. I tired of well-meaning interviewers advising me that I would be great as a social worker, working with the handicapped. They forgot that I might not want to work with the handicapped or return to school. Interviewers were always encouraging, but I never fit into their plans, although they saw me fitting perfectly into someone else's plans. I followed their suggestions, but they always led to a dead end.

An interesting job developed in the program where I was a client. The person who was leaving felt that I would be excellent for the position, and wrote several of my qualifications into the job description, including a graduate degree in marketing. Upon her recommendation, I was to be one of the four people interviewed. I strongly believed that someone in the program should know what it was like to be handicapped.

"What this program does not need is another bureaucratic social worker," the director told me. "Someone with your qualifications could really help this program deal with businesses."

I prepared myself well for the interview.

Walking into the program's office one morning, I listened in shock as a member of the parent organization offered the job to a "bureaucratic social worker" he had just interviewed. The interviewee was an inexperienced woman in her mid-twenties. I had heard that the member of the parent organization that oversaw the program did not give the program much attention or time. The interview that morning had been the first one given.

A woman who already worked in the office was to be one of the four people interviewed, and she was also shocked at what she had heard. We were both upset, not only by the fact that one of us did not get the position, but also by the fact that we were not even interviewed.

I was disillusioned for two weeks, and felt bitter toward the parent organization for their poor handling of the situation. I also felt disappointed for the other clients of the program. There was never any attempt by the organization to talk with the clients about their needs, even though the organization was designed to help disabled clients and administered the Federal funds designated to assist them. The realization that this was not one isolated incident frightened me. *There must be thousands of organizations*, I thought, that treat their clients like *objects*. Frustration drove me out of the program.

I had reached the most difficult part of my recovery: re-entering the mainstream of society. In many ways, I was more alone than at any time since I entered my coma. I was at a standstill; it was depressing and frightening. One would think that lying completely paralyzed, unable to speak or move, would be the most difficult part of my odyssey, but my core values took over at that time almost without effort. Now I had no one to attend to my needs. I did not have nurses rolling me over every two hours to relieve my pain or Lisa reading to me at night, Billy Feathers beating on my chest, or even an intern forcing a feeding a tube down my nostril. Re-entering the mainstream, going to school, dating, getting married, finding a job—that was what really took courage, strength and determination. I had to face failure, let go of my ego, and expose my vulnerabilities and walk onward. Re-entering the mainstream was what we all faced after our personal challenges. I was no different. I was so close, and no one trusted me with any responsibility because of what I had been through.

One stockbroker with whom I talked even suggested that maybe I should think about starting behind the counter at Burger King.

Unsure of how to take more control over my destiny, I wondered how my classmates were doing. Were they working behind the counter at Burger King? I knew differently. My muscles were still stiff, but I had never felt better physically. I had an alertness and sensitivity that I had never had before, but something was holding me back. Was I that different now? Was I looking at the world realistically? I wondered if there was a gap between the way I looked at the world and the way others visualized it. Was that gap somehow holding me back? Was I holding myself back?

My outlook was becoming blurred. I still was grateful to have had my unique experience, but I was starting to be confined on the fringe of society. Running out of money, resources, and energy, I was not happy to be living with my parents in a small Maine town at twenty-eight years old. It was the middle of winter; my parents had gone south. Cold and lonely, I could not seem to take the extra step necessary to move forward. It was a step that I desperately wanted to take.

That step was coming to terms with my new self. I had come a long way since being locked in, but I was not happy with my progress. I looked well on the surface, but in a way that made it all the more difficult. I was hurting inside, and unlike in the past, no one saw my hurt. It was painful for me to compare myself with my friends and relatives who had families of their own, homes, and responsible jobs. They were not a burden on their parents. I had worked hard for an excellent education, but materially it seemed that everyone was doing better than I was. The couple of temporary jobs that I had tried were not a good fit, being physically too demanding. I had overestimated my physical abilities when I took those jobs.

It seemed obvious that I did not fare well when comparing myself to others. Why was that necessary? I had to get my shit together, and fast. I was tired of wallowing in negativity and telling people I was unemployed. That had to change. I focused on what I could do better than ever, not on what I could no longer do. As before, I wanted to learn and grow. My health was going in the right direction, and I had a positive attitude about what I had gained.

Deciding to chronicle my experiences was a major turning point. If nothing else, I would have a legacy for future generations, a gift to my grandchildren, and I owed an explanation to those who had supported me during such difficult times. From that moment on, I had a goal and a purpose.

I had taught in Taiwan, and started to substitute-teach. I loved the high-school kids, the hours fit my schedule, and I was contributing to the community. That led to a permanent teaching position, which laid the foundation for a job with the state government. I met a woman who later became my wife and the mother of my daughter.

Since awaking from the coma, I have been trying to tame the unleashed ball of excitement within me. I often thought of the ball as having demonic qualities, qualities that I could not control, frightening to one who always tried to maintain control. Now, I see that ball of energy and excitement in friendly terms. I have come to terms with myself, I have gained some understanding, but I realize I am far from any real answers.

The more I experience, the more my view of the world expands, and the more elusive the answers appear to be. Instead of discovering truths, they move further from my grasp. People sometimes say, "I guess you can only understand if you've been through it." Having the experience does not mean you understand; it only gives you a different perspective on what you see. The only thing I understand is that I have no answers, and the search for those answers is never-ending. It is like traveling: the more you travel, the greater the realization that there is so much more to see. At last, I am back to life, but my odyssey is just beginning.

## EPILOGUE

It was four thirty in the afternoon when we crossed the Iranian border into No Man's Land on our way to Afghanistan. The sun was lowering in the January sky. Nancy, Dana, and I were in a small minibus with four other international travelers, anxious to leave Iran and hoping to reach Herat, Afghanistan by nightfall.

I had not known this No Man's Land existed, since it did not appear on my maps. It was a ten-mile stretch of semi-arid desert separating the two countries, only occasionally dotted with low-lying bushes. After a long day, all the travelers sat in silence as the rusted minivan pulled into an outpost that appeared abandoned. The turbaned driver disappeared into a building and emerged forty minutes later, saying that the border had closed, and we would have to spend the night in No Man's Land.

The driver led us to an earthen building, and motioned to some beds with rope mattresses where we could unroll our bedding. Then he pointed to an outhouse, and a well where we could wash.

After Nancy, Dana, and I had settled in, we were led to a barren, windowless room where three men with leathery skin and wearing black turbans sat around a gas lantern. Speaking very little English, the Afghans nodded and smiled as they handed us tin plates and spoons. One of the other travelers mumbled something in Dutch as the men served us rice, a dab of vegetables, and a cube of mutton.

Surrounded by the other international travelers, I was excited, not frightened. Had I known about the history of the Khyber Pass, the razor-sharp peaks of the Hindu Kush lit at night by bandits' blazing fires, the religious fanaticism of the Taliban, or Osama Bin Laden's future training camps, I might have thought differently. I looked at those men's hardened faces in the glow of the gas lantern, and there was no doubt I was in a different world than that of the ivy brick walls of Phillips Exeter Academy. Just eighteen, this was the adventure of which I had only dreamed.

Once I crossed into No Man's Land, an exciting new world opened up for me. I was eager to explore. I had no idea what I might learn there that would prepare me for what lay ahead, but I was alive and excited. Little did I know that a few years later I would find myself locked in the No Man's Land of my mind. There was no thought of turning back; I saw that my only choice was to forge ahead into a new world.

Six years later I awoke from a six-week coma, a drooling, sweating, emaciated scarecrow unable to move, blink my eyes, speak, or even swallow. Ruled by uncontrollable spasms, I wasn't about to turn around. Somehow I saw this as another adventure, and ventured forward.

Now, thirty years after waking from the coma, I sit on my deck overlooking the Kennebec River and try to understand the incredible journey I had the opportunity to undertake. I marvel at the soaring bald eagles, the diving osprey, and the leaping sturgeon. Thirty years ago, I asked myself "why me?" nearly every day. I still ask, but it never has a negative connotation. It has been the adventure of a lifetime. Like my trips to Afghanistan and Nepal, or the Philippines and Thailand, it was not always easy or pleasant. There were hardships, thrills and adventures, but I was learning, growing and excited to forge ahead.

Had I continued to be weighed down by Bauby's diving bell, my outlook would no doubt have been different. Had Jean-Dominique Bauby, author of *The Diving Bell and the Butterfly*—an autobiographical account of a locked-in man—been lucky enough to escape from the No Man's Land of his mind, I have no doubt his outlook would have been similar to mine.

I am awed by my odyssey when I view it in a historical perspective, no less than a geographical one. After all, I'm not living in the Dark Ages or in a remote village in Afghanistan. Top-rate medical care was available. As Bauby wrote, it used to be "that people in that condition simply died, now the agony is prolonged," but I was lucky.

Life continues, and I am part of that continuum. I have experienced the miracle of the birth of my daughter. Lisa is now married and has three children of her own. Dean Wilson, who has six grandchildren, has retired from Northwestern Kellogg Business School and is a trustee of Bates College in Maine. Sam, who let Lisa sleep on his floor, just stepped down as a senior vice president of a major corporation, and has two daughters. Anna, my physical therapist, now lives in Massachusetts and has two sons.

My brother John, who used to drive his Le Car with his wife Suellen and their sheepdog from Baltimore to Chicago, now has five kids, two grandkids, and a lobster-processing business which employs 80-100 people. My sister Nancy, who teaches Buddhism and mindfulness, has two sons, and even Bubs, who visited me at the hospital at six months old, has a baby girl. My mother, who lives independently at 91, has eight grandchildren and three great-grandchildren, with more on the way.

Although I started walking with a cane again about ten years ago after an automobile accident, I am healthy and active. Still stiff and slow, I go to Planet Fitness to lift weights and stretch. I dance weekly to live music, am privileged to be able to kayak on the river outside my window, and go at my own slow pace in Tai Chi class. I have even had the opportunity of failing miserably at dancing the Tango in Buenos Aires. I marvel at the power of prayer and meditation, and am fascinated with cooking, maybe because I could not eat for three months.

I often wonder about the events beyond my control while I was lying in a coma. Was I struggling to survive, or had I given up hope? It would be nice to know that I was fighting to survive and that my efforts were rewarded, but I'm not sure that's the case. Was there one critical instance when my life balanced on the knife edge? What prevented me from taking another step into the unknown? Was there one critical moment when my brother's voice or the nurse's warm hand saved my life? I'll never know.

According to a *Men's Health* article, what I experienced was similar to what a hostage might endure. Like a hostage, my brain faced an intensely traumatic situation that activated my hypothalamus to trigger a fight-or-flight reflex. Not being able to fight or flee, I was in a state of anxiety-producing hyper-alertness, and had to resist natural tendencies. Instinctively, I tapped other core elements of my personality, such as patience and self-discipline.

Once I did wake from the coma, I wondered why I recovered as well as I did. Was it pre-determined how far I would return to normal health? Was it just a matter of time? I did have that one trait, resilience, that impacted how I survived and recovered, but that is part of my core deep within me.

When I tell people a brief history of my illness, they often react with shock and horror. "To think it might have been a mosquito," they say in amazement. "God, I'm going to think twice about going outside now."

With a laugh I say, "But you know I am very lucky to have had a chance to experience what I did."

"You mean you feel lucky to have survived?" they ask.

"No, I am lucky to have had such a unique mind-expanding opportunity."

"Come on, you can't mean that," they answer, but I do mean exactly that. Survival may have been at the root of my experience, but it transcended so much more. People shudder when I say I am glad that it happened to me. They give me that sideways glance that means, "Man, are you crazy?" Of course, I am happy with the outcome.

Upon recovering, I had the opportunity to see a rehabilitation film at a head injury support group. The documentary had been well-received nationally. Several patients and their families were interviewed, and the film focused on what the patients could no longer do: a paralyzed athlete who could no longer run the hundred yard dash, a pianist who could no longer play symphonies on the keyboard. Before the film was shown, Kleenex was passed around the room. "A real tearjerker," someone said.

Indeed, after the documentary tears flowed, but I noticed they were not patients' tears. They were shed by family members, and it was the family members who were quick to praise the film. The patients seemed unimpressed but sat quietly, not ready to assert their own opinions.

My point is that patients are always told how to react by people who are looking at the case from an outside perspective. Outsiders always focus on what the patient has lost, not on what the patient has gained. The patient visualizes the world differently than he once did, but he still wants to be a part of the world where he once felt comfortable.

It is hard for me to focus enough on coordination to even dribble a basketball. Undoubtedly, I cannot do what I once found easy, but what I have gained far outweighs what I have lost. I cannot play basketball or softball as I once did, but I enjoy the sunny spring days more than ever before.

The greatest change is my increased sensitivity and compassion towards others. The sensation of my heart expanding throughout my body has had a lasting effect. I have a strong bond toward those who played a role in my survival—not only toward family, doctors, and therapists, but toward friends who prayed for my survival or supported me in other ways. I am not only more aware of others' needs and emotions, I am more capable of seeing the source of their actions and being less judgmental.

More open to a universal scope, I see relationships between objects that were not apparent to me before, and see myself as part of a much larger picture. At the same time, I have greater self-awareness and an inner strength that I lacked before, realizing the impact I can exert over my life. Now, I am more confident to enter into a particular situation, knowing that I can deal with the outcome.

It is too simple to say that I appreciate life more than I once did, but I definitely have a different perspective on it. I cannot adequately describe the feeling of lying totally paralyzed and focusing my energies on each single movement. I cannot describe the thrill of speaking my first words or eating solid food after nearly three months or walking again after never being absolutely sure I would ever be able to do so. They are thrills that I hope I never forget because it makes each word, each bite, each step a little more exciting than it once was.

Lying paralyzed would seem to be a horror, but it was actually the most exciting time in my life. Instinctively, I chose not to focus on lying in pain, drooling, sweating, and coughing uncontrollably. I was not plodding through the workweek waiting for hump day or Friday night. I would fall asleep anticipating the arrival of the next day, and wake each morning after four or five hours' sleep, eager for new developments. I never felt so alive as when I was first regaining movement. Each improvement seemed so monumental, so significant.

What I experienced was traumatic, dramatic, and life-altering, without a doubt. It was not fun being suctioned by a respiratory therapist, lying in a hospital bed unable to move, or now hobbling around with a cane, but life is a series of dramatic events for us all. My event was not necessarily harder for me than it was for Lisa or my mother. I had luck, love, and support, and I flourished. It was exciting to be the focus of so much goodwill and to watch myself progress.

The challenge is to draw a parallel between what I experienced and the tribulations of others. A Japanese koan says life is seven times down, eight times up. The list of possible downs is infinite: the death of a spouse, cancer, depression, bankruptcy, divorce, addiction, or the chronic health problems of a child; these are glaring examples. We all have downs. No one is immune. The seven downs are like a tide, constantly changing and inevitable. I was lucky that my down was very visible to others, and people came to my aid. Love and support transformed my down into an up.

We have a say in our own destiny. We all have the power to change our immediate environment, even if it is only the way in which we view that climate. Life constantly changes. It follows the law of perpetual motion. It may take a mosquito bite or a sledgehammer, but life is going to change.

In Nepal, I met a water buffalo in my path. The Himalayas rose on one side, with a sharp drop-off on the other. I could fight, flee, or forge ahead. We stared at each other for a minute, and I chose to move forward. Luckily, he let me pass, and my life changed, if only a little. I had managed to proceed onward, and laughed at my good fortune. Perhaps the resident who told the interns I would not make it was like that water buffalo, and did me a favor. He was a gatekeeper who gave me the challenge: cower, or proceed with courage. I had escaped death and learned to laugh at my luck much as I did when the water buffalo let me continue on my path. From that moment, I treasured my life like never before. During my odyssey I have shed lots of tears, but I have learned to laugh as well. It's been painful, joyful, intense, and emotional, and I have cried hard, but let it be known that I have laughed harder.

## Brain Research

In order to promote brain research and to support the many individuals who have suffered traumatic brain injury, a portion of the proceeds from each book will be donated to groups such as the International Brain Injury Association and the Brain Research Foundation.